THACKERAY

THACKERAY

A STUDY

BY

ADOLPHUS ALFRED JACK

KENNIKAT PRESS
Port Washington, N. Y./London

THACKERAY

First published in 1895
Reissued in 1970 by Kennikat Press
Library of Congress Catalog Card No: 74-103194
SBN 8046-0831-8

Manufactured by Taylor Publishing Company   Dallas, Texas

TO

MY FATHER,

TO WHOSE ADVICE AND ENCOURAGEMENT IS DUE
ANYTHING OF MERIT IN THIS BOOK.

CONTENTS

THACKERAY: A STUDY.

LIST OF ERRATA.

THACKERAY

INTRODUCTORY

"WE enter on burning ground," says Mr. Arnold in one of those luminous critical essays which are so provocative and so helpful;—"we enter on burning ground as we approach the poetry of times so near to us, poetry like that of Byron, Shelley, and Wordsworth, of which the estimates are so often not only personal, but personal with passion." And that is why, as the great critic has told us, with as much sagacity as iteration, Time is the true test, and the judgments of the High Court are taken, for so wearisome a period, to avizandum. The justice of the remark is never more evident than when we consider the fallibility of contemporary criticism. If the writer has a new gospel to preach, or what looks like a new gospel, there is

the natural alienation of those who prefer the old
order of ideas, or at least the same ideas in their
old setting. If the writer does not pretend to
offer anything new, and openly avows that he
has nothing to say but what has been said before,
only not quite in the same manner, or with quite
the same precision, there is the danger that the
value of his work may be lost sight of, or his
profession of conservatism put down to him as a
want of originality.

But fallible as from its nature contemporary
criticism is, prejudiced and careless as it too
often has been, when contrasted with the criticism
of the decade following the death of a great
writer, when placed side by side with the mean-
ingless phrases that airily condemn, or feebly
prophesy immortality, it assumes the aspect of
sobriety and justice. Contemporary criticism
has at least this merit, that it is an honest
attempt of the critic's own to apportion rewards
and punishments. His hostility may be incurred,
his sympathy may be enlisted, without adequate
cause ; he may not be able to appraise at their
true value all these novel sensations, which a new
and striking work is bound to generate in an
active and reflective mind. In short he may err,

and he may err tremendously, but the error is his own. He may fall a prey to the dangers that beset the contemporary critic, but the critic who is not quite a contemporary is in a still worse position. He is too near not to be open to the same influences which have distracted the judgment of the earlier writer, and he is too apt to be prejudiced not only by the work which he is criticizing, but by the criticisms which have been written upon it. So that in one mood he is tempted servilely to endorse what has been said, in another quite as servilely to contradict it. Add to this that death places an author at the mercy both of enemies and friends, so that it is doubtful whether his memory suffers more from the long-restrained candour of the one class, or the unthinking panegyric of the other, and it will be readily acknowledged that there is no time more unfavourable for arriving at a correct estimate of any writer, than that intervening between his death and the sane decision of posterity.

How long this critical chaos may continue it is quite impossible to say; to attempt to fix for it any particular number of years would be worse than useless. The time fluctuates with quite a surprising variation, and a moment's glance backward at literary history will show us that the comparative greatness of the writer has little to do with the duration of this period of suspense. It is true also, no doubt, that were we to say that we must wait for that judgment till the generation which he has influenced has passed away, this would be to fix too long a time for a few cases, and one far too short for most. But it would at least be safe to say, that when a generation to whom he has not been a contemporary has had time to form its opinions, and has received the works of the author not as an offering peculiarly for itself, but only as a part of the legacy of the past, then it is reasonable to exercise critical opinion about him, and to attempt seriously to ascertain what is, or rather what will be, his ultimate position. As much as this at least may be said, and in particular cases it is possible to say more. If when we look round we find that the author is the object of criticism unimpassioned and painstaking, if we see that on the one hand his faults are admitted, while on the other his excellences are allowed, if we feel that responsible criticism has become cautious and discriminating, these are all proofs that there is fast forming about us a definite and not easily disturbed opinion.

That this is the case with Thackeray, Mr. Trollope's fair and admirable monograph is demonstration enough. It was not to be expected that such a book, published only sixteen years after the death of Thackeray, would be received without murmurs by his disciples, but on the whole the position that has since been accorded to it, the treatment it has received, and indeed the very fact of its existence, are strong evidences of a tendency towards agreement in critical opinion. Thackeray has been dead for thirty-one years, ample time for a generation to spring up for whom, except while they were in the nursery, he was never a living writer. His great contemporary Dickens died in 1870, and George Eliot ten years later ; and it is quite noticeable how different is the attitude of the educated public towards these three names. About Thackeray there is, though not by any means a final, a sufficiently marked consensus of opinion. If it is said that he was a cynic, it is at once admitted that he was too ready to label many of his characters, whose weaknesses he brought into prominence, fool or knave. If it is laid to his charge that he was too much occupied with mean and little things, few who have read the miscellaneous papers and novelettes are prepared to deny it. With Dickens it is another matter. There are some who will not allow that his characters are exaggerated, and there are many who deny to him that gift of pathos on which, equally with his humour, his reputation was at one time supposed to rest. But if there is little agreement about the merits and demerits of Dickens, there is still less about those of George Eliot, and a critic who would attempt to estimate her future position would be but little, if at all, aided by the general opinion.

This at first sight is the more curious, as the genius of Dickens or George Eliot is not at all difficult to understand. There was never any doubt about it in either case. They both achieved distinction by quite different, but by quite simple processes. Dickens, a man of great sensibility, and possessing a fund of humorous description that has in its way never been equalled, took the town by storm by virtue of these qualities. The strong understanding and depth of analytical power which belonged to George Eliot were at once acknowledged as

the causes of her success. Thackeray's genius
was of a more complex order. Alternately
amusing and irritating his generation, at one
moment sneering at those very follies which
at the next set him off into a strain of almost
irresistible tenderness, he presented a problem
to his contemporaries that seemed to admit
of many answers. It is, in reality, precisely
because of the difficulty of the problem that
we may be said already to be within measurable
distance of its solution. It was so impossible
for his contemporaries to agree about this kind-
hearted cynic, this courtier of Queen Anne
who waged unrelenting war against the aristocracy, this fine gentleman who peered into
cupboards, and assessed the price of his enter-
tainment, that the critical intelligence was
thoroughly aroused. There was no one who
was content to read him and be thankful ; there
was not one of his books which did not start
the question :—Who is this man, so many-sided,
so contradictory ? And it was just because this
question was so frequently asked, and so frequently answered, because Thackeray was an
author of such complexity as to force the public
to set themselves to understand him, that his

position in letters has been so quickly and so nearly ascertained.

But it would be a great mistake to suppose that we have yet arrived at anything more than an approximation to the judgment of posterity. We are still far too near for that. Before anything final may be said, or even attempted, by a critic, it is necessary to wait, not only till a new generation shall have grown up to criticize the author, but till a new generation of original writers, who have felt his influence, shall in their turn have had their places apportioned to them, and his influence upon them weighed and appreciated. And so, though the task of the critic of Thackeray is, at the present day, easier than it might have been, it is by no means easy. He will be helped, no doubt, by the prevailing opinion, but he will still have to depend to some extent upon his own intuition, and in a greater degree upon those canons of criticism, by the correct use of which the place of all authors is ultimately decided. Happily there is in general no dispute about the canons; the difficulty lies in their application. The business of criticism being to anticipate the judgment of the world, the obvious course in dealing with any author is to compare him with those upon whom a favourable judgment has already been pronounced. He is to be compared then with the classical authors, and just in so far as he has qualities that are common to the classics, is he likely himself to become classical. There is no disagreement about the classics ; it is the fact of this agreement that gives them their name. We may be said to call only those authors classics whom every one acknowledges to be so.

But though there may be no doubt as to what authors are classical, and as to the fact that the author we are criticizing ought to be compared with them, the question may very well be asked, with what classics he ought to be compared ? A novelist, it may be urged, ought only to be compared with the classical novelist, a romance-writer with the best writers of romance, and a dramatist with Shakespeare or Molière ; to compare a writer with any or all of the classics would not only be tedious but confusing. There is truth in the remark, and no doubt it would be a roundabout way of proving that Tennyson's plays were not well fitted for the stage, to show that Hawthorne's romances possessed a far higher dramatic power, and that there were in 'Queen Mary' and 'Becket' few of the marvellous touches that give to Scott's historical novels an appearance of reality. But that is because we have ready to hand an immense and classical literature written in the form of Tennyson's plays, by comparison with which they can easily be tried. The drama, besides, is almost as old as literature itself. It has portrayed nearly every epoch, it has chronicled nearly every passion, its capacity, if not completely known, has yet had so wide a range that it would be difficult to extend it ; many of the greatest names in the world are the names of dramatists. But the novel is still in its infancy. When one speaks of it, the classical names that rise to one's memory, Cervantes and Le Sage, are not properly those of novelists at all. They came too early for that. Le Sage, indeed, has been called the father or progenitor of the novel, and Fielding, who copied much of his manner, and who wrote immediately afterwards, died within sixty years of Thackeray's birth. That period produced no work of fiction greater than the adventures of Humphry Clinker, and extended to within three years of the production of ' Waverley.' But not only is the novel an essentially modern growth, not only is its province undetermined, so that we apply the name indiscriminately to the adventures of Tom Jones and Roderick Random, the prose dramas of Hawthorne, and the historical romances of Scott,—not only is the novel new and its capacity unknown, but it has not as yet given us many names of the first excellence. Fielding, Scott, Hawthorne ; if we were to try to add anything to that trio we should have to seek among the moderns. Richardson we may dismiss as too little read to be useful for purposes of comparison, and Smollett, where he is not surpassed by Fielding, is purely a humourist.

Thus it would be plainly impossible to test an author who chose to put his writings in the form of a novel by comparing him with other novelists alone. There are so few great names that it becomes necessary to supplement the criterion, and for this purpose we may fairly use the romantic and dramatic fields that are open before us. We may fairly use the romantic, because the distinction between a romance and a novel has never been accurately

drawn. 'The Castle of Otranto,' though its
author is careful to call it a Gothic story, would
probably be classed as a romance, on account of
the supernatural element which it contains ; but
in 'The Mysteries of Udolpho, a romance,' the
mysteries are all finally attributed to natural
causes, and 'The Monastery,' though in its
pages unsparing use was made of the White
Lady, was not for that reason differentiated
from the other novels of the series to which it
belongs. 'The Recess,' by the sisters Lee,
might well be called a romance from the license
which it takes with historical characters, but the
Waverley novels were never supposed to be free
from that fault. A novel, it may be said, deals
with character, but no novel can show more
careful character-drawing than 'The Blithedale
Romance,' and there is nothing more supernatural or romantic in it than a socialistic
community.

And we may fairly use the dramatic field,
because all novels more or less partake of the
character of the drama. A novel, it is almost
needless to say, need not be so dramatic as a
drama. The latter, as it appeals to the eye as
well as to the ear, and has to make its effect in

a much shorter period, depends more upon striking situations. The novel, moreover, has not been subjected to the same extent to the unities of time and place. But many of the greatest dramas have flagrantly broken them, and when all limitations are allowed, it remains true that the qualities that are necessary to produce a good drama are approximately the same qualities that are necessary for a good novel. The object of both is to tell a story, and to tell it in an attractive way; both are occupied with the representation of life and the delineation of character. Not that it follows that a good novel will be easily dramatized, because the situations may not occur at the proper intervals for an adaptation into scenes and acts, they may not be sufficiently frequent or sufficiently pictorial; but in so far as it is a good novel, the situations, when they do occur, must be dramatic enough to leave a definite impress on the mind, the story, when told, must have so much in common with a drama that it can be viewed as a connected whole. The adventures of Gil Blas fail, it is true, when tried by this criterion. Any other series of adventures might equally well have led up to the castle of Lirias and the patent of nobility, and, though the book affords much of the most delightful reading, it is impossible to remember anything more of it than that the hero fell among robbers, spent some time with the actors, and served rather longer with the Count Duke than with the Archbishop of Granada. The book contains enough incident and imagination to make half-a-dozen novels, but it is just because it leaves no definite or connected impression upon the mind that, though it has received the seal of posterity's approbation, and has as much likelihood of immortality as any disconnected story that was ever written, the title of novel has generally been withheld from it.

We have, then, in attempting to estimate the value of Thackeray's works, to keep the example of the great classics constantly before us, the example of those classics, that is, who have occupied themselves with the representation of life. And in making any attempt of the kind, we might at once considerably lighten our task by discarding all those tales and sketches which were written as mere journeyman's work, and which are clearly ephemeral. We might at once, without any compunction, discard ten or

twelve volumes, and at the same time do a real
service to Thackeray, for no author is helped by
having to carry a load of old magazine literature
along with him. By this means we might
lighten our task, but we should probably miss
the object of it. The early works of every
author, his essays and imperfect attempts, are
of considerable service to those who would
understand his character and genius. And of
no author is this more true than of Thackeray.
There have been authors who at a certain period
of their career have entirely changed their
manner of working, so that it would almost
seem that they came to look at the world from
the opposite point of view to that from which
they had started. Thackeray in later life
modified his attitude, but there is no abrupt
transition. One of his latest works was a
rehabilitation of one of his earliest sketches,
and one of the catastrophes in that book of
many catastrophes, 'The Newcomes,' was
borrowed from the turning incident in 'The
Amours of Mr. Deuceace.'[1] The Marquis of

---

[1] Cf. the attack upon Deuceace, by which he lost
his hand, and the duel of which Lord Kew was the
victim.

Farintosh was taken as a peg for the sermon he began to preach in 'The Hoggarty Diamond.' The lot of Catherine, the heroine of his first story, is cast among thieves. Denis Duval, the hero of his last, is the son of a smuggler. The moral of all his earlier stories is to be found in 'Vanity Fair.'

Thackeray had three distinct periods, but they are periods which illustrate each other. First, there is the period before 'Vanity Fair,' the period of his shorter stories, which foreshadow both his first important book, and in a lesser degree 'Pendennis,' 'Esmond,' and 'The Newcomes.' Then there is the period of 'Vanity Fair,' in which he gathered up and used with greater effect all the qualities that had gone to the making of his earlier tales ; and after that there is what may properly be called the period of 'Pendennis,' for it was in 'Pendennis' that he first adopted the larger and humaner manner that was to ripen in 'Esmond' and 'The Newcomes.' But the three periods, though they are quite clearly marked, overlap. In the year in which 'Vanity Fair' was produced, he was still writing 'A Little Dinner at Timmins's,' which appeared as a kind of belated

appendix to ' The Book of Snobs.' The year
that saw the completion of ' Pendennis ' gave
him time to write ' The Kickleburys on the
Rhine,' a story quite in the method of ' Vanity
Fair.'

It follows, then, that a writer like Thackeray,
who is throughout his career so true to himself,
cannot properly be judged by samples. There
is no book of his so bad that it does not bear
some likeness to his best, and but one so good
that it does not remind the reader of how far
from his best it was possible for him to fall
away. Concealed behind an attitude that varies
from pity to mockery, and from mirth to tears,
hid behind a multitude of characters in reality
astonishingly diverse, there lies a sameness so
provoking that there remains nothing which it
is allowable to discard. Thackeray was a man-
nerist, and of most mannerists one book is as
good as all. He, almost alone, was the possessor
of a manner which, though seldom varying in
essentials, abounds in variety. Between his
best book and his worst there is a surprising
distance. With most authors who have left a
body of work of widely differing degrees of

excellence, it is possible to discard something; he, almost alone, remains amid his differences essentially the same.   To borrow a phrase from Mr. Arnold, "the real Thackeray" is not to be found by any process of selection.

CHAPTER I

BEFORE 'VANITY FAIR'

FEW authors have suffered more than Thackeray from the republication of stories that would not live by themselves; but the industry of disciples must stop somewhere, and the twenty-four volumes already published do not contain all that he wrote. Neither the title nor the subject of his first story are known, but he appears in a drawing of Maclise's, as one of the contributors to 'Fraser' in 1835, and before that he wrote for, and lost much money by, a transitory paper called 'The National Standard.' But the first work of any importance upon which we find him engaged is 'The Memoirs of Mr. C. J. Yellowplush, sometime footman in many genteel families.' There are two tales worth notice in the Memoirs, 'Miss Shum's Husband,' and 'The Amours of Mr. Deuceace.'

The hero of the first is a crossing-sweeper by profession, who plays the gentleman of small means in the evening, at a tumble-down lodging in John Street. The backbone of the story is a situation of which Thackeray did not weary till the period of Pendennis, the situation, in some form or other, of Cinderella and her sisters. It is a comparatively simple way of providing a heroine, all that is necessary being to place a spiritless and amiable young woman amid vulgar surroundings. However uninteresting in herself, she excites interest by virtue of the juxtaposition. It is the wicked sisters that make us desire the prince for the little kitchen-wench, not the humility with which she receives their blows. The character of Mary Shum, as that of Caroline in the 'Shabby Genteel Story,' is hardly drawn at all; they shine, where everything else is vulgar and mean, not by their virtues but by their nothingness. Many years later, in a far longer story, Thackeray tried to arouse interest in Amelia by contrasting her with Becky, and when this was found to be insufficient, by vulgarizing the characters of her parents. But it is easy to see that he grew tired of the negative doll he had created, and, from

his not recurring to the artifice after 'Vanity
Fair,' that he came to acknowledge his mistake.
The truth is that if we consent to be interested
in Cinderella, it is because the story is so slight
that we never take the trouble to analyze the
character at all. The artifice, though it may
pass in a sketch, is quite unsuited for a work
of a more important kind. Puppets, no doubt,
have been introduced into the greatest works of
imagination, but it is not for the purpose of
shining. On the contrary, it is that they may
afford a background from which the more
brilliant characters may stand out in relief. For
the rest, Mr. Yellowplush tells his story with
much of that humour which consists in bad
spelling and the alliance of pretentiousness and
poverty.

'The Amours of Mr. Deuceace' is an effort
of a more ambitious nature. It is the story of
the career of a gambler, considerably more
highly placed in society than Mr. Yellowplush's
last master, but possessing none of the advan-
tages that rank and education are supposed to
confer. The portrait is said to be drawn from
nature, Thackeray having actually been the
"pigeon" of the tale ; but for the subsequent

career of Mr. Deuceace, recourse has been had
to the imagination. The story is told with great
skill. We find ourselves following, with close
attention, the career of a number of characters,
in not one of whom we have the least interest.
We are glad when Mr. Deuceace steals his four
thousand pounds, we are quite satisfied that he
should be maimed, and we rather enjoy the
triumph which his worthless parent finally gains
over him. The story, which was meant to be
highly moral, is written in so low a tone that it
is difficult to have a moral idea in connection
with it. Mr. Dawkins is a foolish snob, Mr.
Blewitt is as unprincipled as Mr. Deuceace, and
the Earl of Crabs is the despicable prototype of
the Marquis of Steyne. Of the female characters one is merely unfortunate and contemptible, but the other hunts for a title and attempts
a murder. And even Mr. Yellowplush betrays
the interests of his rascally employer. There is
nothing for the mind to rest upon except the
conflicting schemes of the disreputable crew,
but so well is the story told that though we are
indifferent as to which of the schemes is
ultimately successful, we retain our interest in
the dénouement. Thackeray's intention was to

show that the profession of the gambler was as hurtful to himself as to his associates ; but in his effort to effect this he so crowded his canvas with vice and folly that he left little room for the moral sentiments to have play, and the chief impression we derive from the book is that Mr. Deuceace was no worse than his neighbours.

The most remarkable thing about the two stories is the extraordinary care and patience with which the meanest actions are portrayed, and the absence of any sentiment more generous than the reflection of the runaway footman, with which the second story closes—

" Deuceace turned round. I see his face now —the face of a devvle of hell ! First he lookt towards the carridge and pinted to it with his maimed arm ; then he raised the other, and struck the woman by his side. She fell, scream- ing. Poor thing, poor thing ! "

Surely no moralist ever made a more unfortu- nate start than Thackeray with ' The Memoirs of Mr. Yellowplush.'

In the next year or two there appeared another story of a somewhat similar character, which is open in some degree to the same objections.

It also was written with an avowed purpose, and as the purpose was not so definite as that which inspired 'The Amours of Mr. Deuceace,' and indeed was almost banal in its simplicity, it sufficiently served the object of the author. Bulwer Lytton and Harrison Ainsworth had attracted the attention of the public with novels of the class of 'Eugene Aram,' 'Dick Turpin,' and 'Jack Sheppard,' and at the same time had excited the indignation of Thackeray, who was anxious to show to the world how "disgusting would be the records of thieves, cheats, and murderers, if their doings and language were described according to their nature, instead of being handled in such a way as to create sympathy, and therefore imitation." [1] The result was a story in which thieves and murderers were shown to be commonly very bad people indeed, and if the proposition could ever have been doubted, he may be said to have proved it. At the end of 'Catherine,' he makes Ikey Solomons, its supposed author, remark, "Be it granted Solomons is dull, but don't attack his morality." The wonder is that he should ever have thought it necessary to use such language

[1] Trollope's 'Thackeray.'

in connection with it. The tendency of the
story is not immoral,—the tendency of nothing
that Thackeray ever wrote was immoral,—but
neither is it moral. It was written to serve a
moral purpose, but there is no opportunity in
the whole of it for the exercise of morality. To
say that there are some completely bad people
in the world is not to utter a moral sentiment, it
is merely to be guilty of a slightly uncharitable
truism. Nor is it immoral for Shakespeare to
refuse to paint Macbeth as wholly black, or for
Scott to give to Rob Roy the qualities of courage
and magnanimity. To give to a man who commits murder some of the finer feelings was no
more a fault in Lytton ; and Ainsworth was
entitled to assume that a man might be a high-
wayman and at the same time dashing and
debonair. Eugene Aram no doubt is a stilted
character, and the almost forgotten romances of
' Jack Sheppard ' and ' Dick Turpin ' have now
few admirers left. If in them vice was painted
so as to allure, though it is difficult to imagine
what reasonable being could have been allured
by them, in so far they were immoral. But
they were not immoral because they gave a
medley of faults and excellences to the same

character, any more than 'Catherine' is moral merely because it depicts vice in unattractive colours ; if that were so the 'Newgate Calendar' would be a moral production. Morality does not exist by the mere absence of immorality. In books, it is by the reasoned alternation of good and evil that the moral effect is produced.

Faithful to the object with which he set out, Thackeray has enlivened the prevailing sombreness of 'Catherine' with few redeeming traits of character, and the latter half of the book is too sordid for the purposes of fiction ; but the tale, as Mr. Trollope has remarked, is rendered tolerable by the art with which it is narrated. There are few more characteristic bits of irony to be found in Thackeray than Count Galgenstein's reception of his offspring, and the saturnine playfulness with which the career of Captain Brock is chronicled, was the same that enabled his creator, five years afterwards, to write that 'Jonathan Wild' of the nineteenth century, 'The Memoirs of Barry Lyndon.'

But 'Catherine' and 'The Memoirs of Mr. Yellowplush' were not the only result of the four years between 1837 and 1841. With that indolent industry for which he was famous,

Thackeray poured out a succession of sketches and novelettes, only two of them, however, 'A Shabby Genteel Story' and 'The Great Hoggarty Diamond,' possessing more than a biographical interest.

'The Tremendous Adventures of Major Gahagan' are nearly as broad farce as those of Baron Munchausen. The story is parody all through, and even the artifice of exactness, by which in the most preposterous tale an impression of truth is conveyed, comes in for its share of caricature. "I aimed so true," says the Major, "that one hundred and seventeen best Spanish olives were lodged in a lump in the face of the unhappy Loll Mahommed." 'The Fatal Book' and 'Cox's Diary' are also humorous efforts. There is some resemblance between the two stories, and it is satisfactory that in the treatment of the later there is a distinct advance in good-nature. There is a certain harshness in our being invited to laugh broadly at the accumulated misfortunes of the idiot Stubbs, and his treatment of his mother is too wicked to be in keeping with his farcical character. But the ups and downs of Mr. Cox, and his final anchorage in a station suited to him, are a justifiable subject for humour. With the happy philosophy that induces Mr. Cox to acknowledge that " he is like the Swish people, and can't flourish out of his native hair," and with his daughter comfortably paired with Mr. Crump, the comical barber can afford to let us laugh at his many absurdities.

'The Bedford Row Conspiracy' is a more serious tale, that brings little credit to its author. The plot, which was borrowed, is extremely unfortunate, the happiness of the young couple being brought about by a trick which does not deserve a reward. The dramatis personæ are nearly all self-seeking nonentities, and the gravity of the charges preferred against society in the tale is quite out of proportion to its importance. Forty pages suffice to tell us that there are old women without dignity, and young women without reserve, that there is nothing unusual in two old people keeping an assignation, or in a small bevy of men and women of all ages listening at a keyhole, that there are many toadies and liars in the world, and that political life is corrupt. 'Captain Rook' and 'The Fashionable Authoress' are studies of the same class. We learn here also that there are many people who swindle, and many who are swindled, and an additional fact, which does not indeed surprise us, that if an author or authoress has rank or power, their productions are not likely to be less favourably reviewed.

'The Paris Sketch-Book' is a more remarkable production. It is a curious but instructive medley of tales, translations, and reflections. Here we find every mood of Thackeray's young days represented, and the critic who would understand what kind of man it was who wrote 'Barry Lyndon' and 'Vanity Fair' has no more to do than to study it. The same hand which drew Messrs. Cox and Dawkins drew Mr. Pogson. The same taste that made it possible to write 'Catherine,' was responsible for Cartouche and the story of Mary Ancel. The same moralizing tendency which made Thackeray indignant with Bulwer Lytton, dictated the review of the fashionable novels of France. The same feeling that gives its pathos to the homely little tragedy in the 'Hoggarty Diamond,' led him to write the charming morality of Beatrice Merger, and gave occasion for the attack on George Sand. The gambler's death-bed is reminiscent of Mr. Deuceace, and the same cynicism which induced him to chronicle the pity of Mr. Yellowplush, puts an epitaph into the mouth of the landlady.

It is with some feelings of curiosity that we turn to the last paper in the book. Here surely ('Meditations at Versailles') we shall find something new. The palace of the greatest monarchy of modern times must surely awaken other reflections than a druggist out for a holiday,[1] a swindler,[2] or a thief.[3] Here at least have been men as great, and feelings and passions as ennobling, as any in the world. But our expectations are doomed to be disappointed. Amid the crowd of its memories, what arrests his attention is that the courtiers desert Louis XV. on his death-bed, as meaner servants desert their masters ; and the Grand Monarque himself gives rise to no other idea, than that as a journeyman may be tricked out to pass for a gentleman, so a puppet may be painted and padded to look like a king. "It is curious," he writes, "to see how much precise majesty there is in that figure

[1] Mr. Pogson, in 'A Caution to Travellers.'
[2] The Hon. A. P. Deuceace, in 'The Amours of Mr. Deuceace.'
[3] Mr. Macshane, in 'Catherine.'

of Ludovicus Rex. In the plate opposite we
have endeavoured to make the exact calculation.
The idea of kingly dignity is equally strong in
the two outer figures ; and you see at once that
majesty is made out of the wig, the high-heeled
shoes, and cloak all fleurs-de-lis bespangled. As
for the little, lean, shrivelled, paunchy old man
of five feet two, in a jacket and breeches, there
is no majesty in him at any rate ; and yet he
has just stepped out of that very suit of clothes.
Put the wig and shoes on him, and he is six feet
high ;—the other fripperies, and he stands before
you majestic, imperial, and heroic ! Thus do
barbers and cobblers make the gods that we
worship."

When this is the treatment that Louis XIV.
receives, it is no matter for surprise that the
Second Funeral of Napoleon should not awake
in Thackeray any sentiments of admiration or
of awe, but that he should feel himself impelled
to write a burlesque account of the ceremony is
more than the ' Meditations at Versailles ' had
given us reason to expect. The ' Meditations
at Versailles ' were certainly not those to which
we should have anticipated the place would give
birth, but the criticisms upon Louis XIV., when

made, are quite easy to·understand. Great as
he was, Louis was more the centre of a vast
system than the creator of it ; the throne that
was his by right of birth was already one of
the most distinguished in Europe, and it is
historically true that not only was his court a
court of pomp and parade, but also that an
excessive respect was paid to the central figure
within it. The criticism is an unjust caricature,
but had the paper been entitled ' Meditations
upon Louis XIV.,' that would have been all that
was to be said about it.

None of the circumstances, however, which
go to justify in a slight degree his references to
Louis XIV. assist us to explain his attitude
regarding Napoleon. Napoleon began life as a
private man ; he is not only the central figure
in the nineteenth century, but he was the creator
of modern France. His court was more like the
head-quarters of a general than the seat of a
king, and there was no more pomp and parade
in it than is inseparable from any court, ancient
or modern. There is no story more splendid in
history than that of his rise and fall. It was
politically necessary after Waterloo that his
people should desert him, but the fact of their

desertion remains. He might well be excused if he imagined, as he was sinking to an undistinguished grave in St. Helena, that the country for which he had done so much had treated him with ingratitude.

It was not till nearly twenty years afterwards, when the political aspect of affairs had changed, that his countrymen determined to testify, as best they could, their regard for his memory. The means that suggested itself was to provide a more honourable sepulture for his remains. The preparations may have been insufficient, but there could hardly have been an occasion more solemn. From Austerlitz to St. Helena, from St. Helena to the Invalides,—there have been few careers, or few reputations, with transitions more abrupt, few that could better furnish a text for a sermon on the evanescent character of existence, or point more sharply the contrast between the ambitious achievements of man and the essential nothingness of his busy and anxious life.

But Thackeray, from the time when the expedition sets out, under the command of the Prince de Joinville, to the time when, " My dear Miss Smith, the great Napoleon was buried,"

D

assails the ceremony with ridicule. At the
grave at St. Helena, indeed, he allows another
to tell the story, but at the Invalides he has no
such reticence. The procession is described as
if it were a scene from a pantomime, and the
narrative is interspersed with such stage directions as, " Enter a fat priest who bustles up to
the drum-major," or such curiously *mal à propos*
reflections as, " The very fact of a squeeze dissi-
pates all solemnity "; but he reserves the brunt
of his raillery for the effigy that surmounted the
funeral car. If it were usual to be critical in
such things, it is probable that the effigy was a
mistake ; but surely it is not usual to find a fit
subject for ridicule in the trappings of a hearse.
This is how Thackeray writes of it :—" His
Majesty the Emperor and King reclined on his
shield, with his head a little elevated. His
Majesty's skull is voluminous, his forehead broad
and large. We remarked that his Imperial
Majesty's brow was of a yellowish colour, which
appearance was also visible about the orbits of
the eyes. He kept his eyelids constantly closed,
by which we had the opportunity of observing
that the upper lids were garnished with eye-
lashes. Years and climate have effected upon the

face of this great monarch only a trifling alteration ; we may say indeed that Time has touched
his Imperial and Royal Majesty with the lightest
feather in his wing. In the nose of the Conqueror
of Austerlitz we remarked very little alteration ;
it is of the beautiful shape which we remember
it possessed five-and-twenty years since, ere
unfortunate circumstances induced him to leave
us for a while. The nostril and the tube of the
nose appear to have undergone some slight
alteration, but in examining a beloved object
the eye of affection is perhaps too critical. Vive
l'Empereur! the soldier of Marengo is among
us again."

Thackeray has his own excuse for this treatment of the subject. He protests, in effect, that
one may ridicule the funeral without ridiculing
the dead. No doubt it is perfectly possible, but
Thackeray has not attempted to do it. He does
not, it is true, ridicule the career of Napoleon,
because even with his talents for caricature the
task was quite beyond his capacity, but he
ridicules Napoleon through his funeral. And
even if we allow his excuse, there was nothing
ridiculous in the funeral itself. If the pomp
were not sufficiently magnificent to satisfy M.

Thiers, Thackeray would not have had it more so ; and if he would, the fact that the preparations were insufficient did not add to the humour of the occasion. The humour, on his own confession, must have consisted either in the removal of the body, or in its not being removed as quietly as possible. Reduced to this, the subject does not appear as particularly laughable ; but the truth of the matter is, that Thackeray, all through his life, was absolutely incapable of being impressed with those ideas of grandeur and majesty that produce so great an effect upon the rest of the world. In his later years there were none so quick to seize on the grandeur of simplicity, there were none who had a profounder idea of the majesty of virtue. Greatness, beauty, unselfishness ;—all the qualities which go to make a grand character, these he understood and admired. Before the sacredness of prayer, before a character as courageous and as simple as Scott's, he was the first to bow the knee ; but he seems never to have known what is meant by the word magnificent, or to have been dazzled by what is famous and splendid in life.[1] His Prince in 'Esmond' is

[1] Cf., for an instance of this, his treatment of Rome,

royal, but he is not majestic ; and he judges of
the four Georges as if they were English squires.
He had an absolute genius for the historical
novel, but it was the historical novel of private
life. He never introduces us to a monarch, and
hardly gets nearer a court than to tell us that
Beatrix was a maid-of-honour, and that Captain
Brock was presented. He was no chronicler of
princes, and he seems with such labour to have
come to the conclusion that a monarch is a man,
that he resents the distinctions which a throne
and a crown create. The same feelings are
noticeable when he speaks of the petty princes
of Germany, or of our landed aristocracy. The
possession of a coronet is enough to provoke
his resentment. At the idea of majesty all his
hostility is incurred ; he begins at once to laugh
or to sneer. When he comes to deal with the
majestic and terrible Swift, he does not laugh
indeed,—who could laugh at that tragedy ?—he
is even surprised into an involuntary expression
of admiration :—" So great a man he seems to
me, that thinking of him is like thinking of an

---

in the thirty-fifth chapter of ' The Newcomes,' with
Hawthorne's, in the eleventh chapter of the second
volume of ' The Marble Faun.'

empire falling,"—but the larger part of his essay is occupied in sneering at his religion, and misjudging his genius; and he drags him into 'Esmond'[1] that he may call him a bully and a coward.

It would indeed have been remarkable had it been otherwise. Had Thackeray been dazzled by the greatness of Louis XIV. or Napoleon, his character would have been even more complex than it is. Scott, it has been said with great critical truth, was equally at his ease with George IV. or Adam Purdie, equally at home with Queen Mary[2] or Jeanie Deans.[3] The same man that, in 'Twenty Years After,' gave us Charles II. at the Hague, was able to depict with a charming tenderness of observation the bourgeois qualities of Goodman Buvat.[4] It is a commonplace that princes and peasants absolutely jostle each other in the pages of Shakespeare. But none of these authors ever drew anything that was merely squalid. Shakespeare has not the word in his vocabulary. The cabin of Meg Merrilees has none of the comforts of

[1] 'Esmond,' Book iii., chap. v.
[2] 'The Abbot.'
[3] 'The Heart of Midlothian.'
[4] 'Le Chevalier d'Harmenthal.'

civilization, but who would hesitate to affirm
that it is infinitely less contemptible and mean
than the surroundings of Caroline Gann?
Dumas, Scott, or Shakespeare would not have
understood, or if they had understood would
have scorned to chronicle, the doings of the
household which forms the subject of 'A
Shabby Genteel Story.' From the cottage to
the palace is only a step, but for the man who
could look with unblinking eyes on the vulgar
wickedness of Firmin,[1] on the vulgar passion of
Fitch,[1] on the vulgar maternity of Mrs. Gann,[1]
Solomon in all his glory was no more than the
naked Prince in the fairy tale, who, every one
else thought, was clothed in the garments of
majesty.

It would be difficult to find anything favourable to say of the book in which these persons
appear. The reader may consent to be interested
in the scheming wretches who surround Mr.
Deuceace, and even in 'Catherine' the characters,
once we allow that they will stick at nothing,
act much as other selfish people do who have
only their own ends to gain; but in 'A Shabby
Genteel Story' the atmosphere is impregnated

---

[1] 'A Shabby Genteel Story.'

with a vulgarity so intense as to be brutal, and the laugh with which the sordid story is recounted jars in our ears. It is not that satire offends ; it is that the methods of this satirist are offensive. Mankind, it may almost be said, appreciates abuse. The indignation that runs riot among the Yahoos forces us to receive the lesson in a thankful, if in a sorrowing spirit. We confess in church every Sunday that we are miserable sinners, and say over again the wonderful and penitent sentence that embraces the whole catalogue of crimes. But the lesson is accepted, and the admission is made, with anger and tears. Swift, it has been said, never threw filth except when he was angry. The remark is profound ; and we turn to demand from Thackeray what right he had to bring us into such company, unless he were very angry indeed. The gibe of the satirist is forgiven, because of the curse that follows and explains it ; but a laughter that has no pity in its mockery, that is neither merry nor scornful, cannot be forgiven, because it cannot be understood. No man ever rose from reading ' Gulliver's Travels ' without being either wiser or better. We close the ' Shabby Genteel Story ' with a shudder, because we dare not allow ourselves to be ashamed of our species.

It was at this period of Thackeray's life, just after the completion of this story, that his great sorrow befell him ; and the increased tenderness of some passages in ' The Great Hoggarty Diamond ' may, no doubt, be traced to this cause. It was written at a time, he says in one of his letters, " when my heart was very soft and humble. Ich habe auch viel geliebt." But though this influence is noticeable, the manner remains very much the same. We are introduced again to " shabby-genteel " society, and there is quite the usual proportion of fools and knaves in the book. The plot is sufficiently simple. A young clerk has his head turned by the gift of a diamond pin, which not only draws attention to him but induces him to live rather beyond his small means. This leads through the debtor's prison, and his wife's going out as a nurse, to the ultimate resuscitation of their small fortunes by the generosity of her employer. Partly because of the period at which it was written, and partly because there is to be found in it Thackeray's first serious attempt at the pathetic, the story has received much higher praise than it deserves. The characters are not drawn with a firm enough hand to provoke disgust, but it is only their insignificance that saves them. Mr. Brough, a pompous promoter of bubble companies, Miss Hoggarty, a quite incon-sistent old harridan, Gus Hawkins, a singularly rough piece of honesty, and the Misses Brough, who talk French and affect the airs of fashion, form the nucleus of a society whose acquaintance few would care to possess. Mr. Titmarsh himself is not a peculiarly attractive person, and his nick-name, "the West-Ender," gives a fair idea of the company which he frequents. The story is further garnished with a caricature portrait of an aristocratic *ménage*, and winds up with the unnecessary incident of a frivolous attempt at seduction. But even with these unpromising materials, Thackeray has contrived to write a comparatively readable novel, and the troubles of Mr. Titmarsh and his young wife are told with some traces of that feeling which is so prominent a feature of his later work. " It was not, however," writes the autobiographical Titmarsh, " destined that she and her child should inhabit that little garret. We were to leave our lodgings on Monday morning ; but on

Saturday evening the child was seized with convulsions, and all Sunday the mother watched and prayed for it ; but it pleased God to take the innocent infant from us, and on Sunday, at midnight, to lay it a corpse on its mother's bosom. Amen. We have other children, happy and well, now round about us, and from the father's heart the memory of this little thing has almost faded ; but I do believe that every day of her life the mother thinks of the first-born that was with her so short a while : many and many a time has she taken her daughter to the grave, in Saint Bride's, where he lies buried ; and she wears still at her neck a little, little lock of gold hair, which she took from the head of the infant as he lay smiling in his coffin. It has happened to me to forget the child's birthday, but to her never ; and often, in the midst of common talk, comes something that shows she is thinking of the child still,—some simple allu-. sion that is inexpressibly affecting."

Two other papers, 'Going to see a Man hanged' and an article on George Cruikshank, were also the product of this busy period. As to the former, there was no particular reason why Thackeray should have mixed himself up with a controversial question, the different sides of which he does not appear to have studied. But the paper contains some graphic description, and represents fairly the popular view of the time. The review on Cruikshank was a kind office to an artist who was in danger of being neglected, and it is quite remarkable how, when he leaves fiction, he lays aside his prejudices, and his heart begins to expand. The article is full of discriminating, if lenient criticism, and a kindliness that in doing honour to Cruikshank does equal honour to its author. Even the spirited illustrations to the hated 'Jack Sheppard' come in for their full measure of praise ; and every one who has had in his hand the queer old romances of Pierce Egan, and remembers what they were to our grandfathers, will appreciate the wise charity of the references to Bob Logic and Corinthian Tom. Seldom has an appeal for a brother genius been put more delicately or better than this :—

"What labour has Mr. Cruikshank's been ! Week by week, for thirty years, to produce something new ; some smiling offspring of painful labour, quite independent and distinct from its ten thousand jovial brethren ; in what hours of

sorrow and ill-health to be told by the world,
'Make us laugh or you starve—Give us fresh
fun ; we have eaten up the old and are hungry.'
And all this he has been obliged to do—to
wring laughter day by day, sometimes, perhaps,
out of want, often certainly from ill-health or
depression—to keep the fire of his brain per-
petually alight ; for the greedy public will give
it no leisure to cool.   This he has done, and
done well.   He has told a thousand truths in as
many strange and fascinating ways ; he has
given a thousand new and pleasant thoughts to
millions of people ; he has never used his wit
dishonestly ; he has never, in all the exuberance
of his frolicsome humour, caused a single painful
or guilty blush ; how little do we think of the
extraordinary power of this man, and how
ungrateful we are to him ! "

More than twelve years afterwards, he was
occupied in doing a similar service for Leech,
but the later article, though excellent, as was all
the work of that period, does not exceed the
former in grace.   Neither paper pretends to be
a complete critical estimate of its subject.   They
both remain as perfect examples of the manner
in which to teach a careless public how to admire.

Much of the same good-nature is evident in
' The Confessions and Professions of Mr. Fitzboodle,' the least unimportant of the stray
works which occupied 1842. George Fitzboodle
is a man about town, and his confessions are the
narrative of the love-affairs of his youth.   He
introduces himself with much *bonhomie*:—
"What is the simple deduction to be drawn
from this truth?"—the truth that Mr. Fitzboodle was more than a match for "these
literary fellows"—"Why, this—that a man to
be amusing and well-informed has no need of
books at all, and had much better go to the
world and to men for his knowledge.   There
was Ulysses, now, the Greek fellow engaged in
the Trojan war, as I dare say you know.   Well,
he was the cleverest man possible, and how?
From having seen men and cities, their manners
noted and their realms surveyed, to be sure.
So have I.   I have been in every capital, and
can order a dinner in any language in Europe."
It is in this spirit that Mr. Fitzboodle rattles
on, with no very clear idea of the distinction in
things, but always self-satisfied and jovial.   It
is a style which admirably suits the little
historiettes of Mary, Dorothea, and Ottilia.

With great self-complacency he tells us how he
lost Mary on account of his affection for
tobacco, Dorothea through a disastrous tumble
at a ball, and Ottilia because he discovered that
she was a glutton. Besides this, there are
glimpses of the court of Pumpernickel, and
some of Ottilia's peculiarities were reproduced
in Blanche Amory. Blanche also ate too much,
but unlike Ottilia she had the sense to do it in
private, and Ottilia scribbles verses that if they
were not so good would remind us of 'Mes
Larmes':—

"Ah, happy childish tales—of knight and faërie !
  I waken from my dreams—but there's never a knight
    for me.
  I waken from my dreams—and wish that I could be
  A child by the old hall fire—upon my nurse's knee."

The character is well kept up in the ridiculous
'Professions,' and fairly preserved in 'Mr. and
Mrs. Frank Berry,' but it is difficult to imagine
what induced Thackeray to credit Mr. Fitzboodle with the authorship of 'The Ravenswing.' The humorous idler who is at once the
historian and the hero of his own trifles had no
motive for telling it, and a club-lounger could
not have had any knowledge of the society

which it professes to depict.   There is no reason
for attempting to deny what is so palpable, that
the novel was written by the author of 'A
Shabby Genteel Story' and 'The Great Hoggarty Diamond.'   The story is sad enough in
itself.   Morgiana Crump, the daughter of the
landlord of the Bootjack, refuses both the selfish,
though passionately devoted Eglantine, and the
genuine Mr. Woolsey, preferring the attractions
of a certain Captain Walker, whose name does
not appear in the Army List.   She pays the
penalty of her folly, and her husband, who lives
on her voice, and turns out to be a swindler and
a bankrupt, returns her affection with ill-usage.
It is only in a postscript that we are told that
she lived to survive him, and passed the re-
mainder of her days as the respectable Mrs.
Woolsey.   The characters, good, bad, and indifferent (and there is only one that is good),
are so deplorably vulgar as to become, long
before the end of the book, intolerably wearisome.   But that is not how Thackeray regards
them.   To him they are a constant source of
amusement, and their escapades and misfortunes
amazingly diverting.   He tells us that Mrs.
Crump was a retired ballet-dancer, and to him

it is an excellent joke ; that Mr. Woolsey was a tailor, and for him thenceforward his virtues are merely an occasion for ridicule ; that Mr. Eglantine was a hairdresser, and he bids us agree with him that it is the funniest thing in the world.   Indeed, so uncontrollably merry is he, that we are constrained to laugh in spite of ourselves ; but we pause to consider whether we have laughed at a man for being a tradesman, or at a tradesman for falling in love.   The next story, 'Dennis Hoggarty's Wife,' has a widely different treatment accorded to it.   It is a short and gruesome study of the relations between an honest simpleton and the worthless woman whom he has married, but it hardly repays the trouble of reading, and throws no new light on Thackeray's character.

The same remark might almost be made about 'The Irish Sketch-Book,' which, however, of its kind is exceedingly well done.   But guide-books and itineraries, be they ever so industrious and painstaking, must of their nature have little interest, except for the generation for which they are written.   Wordsworth's 'Guide to the Lake District,' no doubt, will continue to be read, but then not only is it a model of

E

English classical prose, but it contains some of the most philosophical reflections upon scenery that have ever appeared.   But from the information that was amassed in 'The Irish Sketch-Book,' Thackeray seldom takes the trouble to derive a general conclusion, and there are none of those wide disquisitions upon society and government, which the investigation of a particular country suggests to writers of the class of De Tocqueville and M. Taine.   It is not easy even to get an accurate idea from it of his views on Ireland itself.   At one moment he seems to incline to the opinion that there is a large class in a state of apparently helpless poverty, at another to the more optimistic one, that the country was generally advancing, and that we had good reason to hope for the best.   There is a legend that he wrote a preface for the second edition, advocating the disestablishment of the Irish Church, and the repeal of the Union.[1] This preface, however, has not appeared.   If it was ever written, it must have fitted in oddly with some other parts of the work.   But though ' The Irish Sketch-Book ' has few attractions for

[1] ' The Life of Thackeray,' p. 117, Great Writers Series. Herman Merivale and Frank T. Marzials.

the general reader, neither the traveller nor the historian can afford to neglect it ; and there are many passages which help the critic of Thackeray's novels more thoroughly to understand his treatment of the Irish.

'Little Travels and Roadside Sketches,' though only about a tenth part of the length, is also very much of a guide-book, but the author is more inclined to moralize upon what he observes, and here and there there is a touch of his ironical manner. " An instance of honesty," he remarks, " may be mentioned with applause. The writer lost a pocket-book containing a passport and a couple of modest ten-pound notes. The person who found the portfolio ingeniously put it into the box of the post-office, and it was faithfully restored to the owner ; but somehow the two ten-pound notes were absent. It was, however, a great comfort to get the passport and the pocket-book, which must be worth about ninepence." And again, writing of his doings at the Hospital of Bruges, " The box-bearer did not seem at first willing to accept our donation— we were strangers and heretics ; however, I held out my hand, and he came perforce as it were. Indeed it had only a franc in it ; but *que voulez-*

vous ? I had been drinking a bottle of Rhine wine that day, and how was I to afford more ? The Rhine wine is dear in this country, and costs four francs a bottle." The writer who spoke in this tone of the motives that prompted his own good actions, was not likely, when he came to more serious work, to be much impressed with the feelings that are responsible for the little kindnesses of everyday life.

In 1844, when Thackeray was forty-one years of age, ' Barry Lyndon ' was published ; and ' The Next French Revolution,' a burlesque which appeared about the same time, is interesting, though a trifle, as showing how completely he had caught the art of telling a fictitious story with a semblance of truth. The seriousness of the narrator is preserved in a wonderful manner, and the attitude maintained throughout is one of judicial calm. But the incidents are so intentionally monstrous that no skill could induce us even for a moment actually to believe in them. Barry Lyndon's adventures, on the contrary, though it is true they are not the most probable, do not exceed the bounds of probability ; and the art, which is conspicuous in ' The Next French Revolution,' is here in such complete perfection, that under its spell we would have no hesitation in believing a tale fifty times less probable. Here indeed we have "old friends with new faces." Over and over again Thackeray had shown the public that out of the most unfortunate materials he could construct a story that would interest, even when it did not please, and that would amuse even when it excited disgust. But no one was ever disgusted at 'The Memoirs of Barry Lyndon.' It is as pleasant a story of its kind as ever excited the mirth, or absorbed the interest of a reader. Already he had shown that he had patience to deal with every species of rascal, and with every variety of vice, a patience so vast indeed that in many cases it exceeded that of his audience. But Redmond Barry might recount his rascalities for ever, and his audience would only be thankful. Often he had told us that gambling was a vice, that mercenary marriages invariably led to misfortune, and that brutality was almost a crime ; but we scarcely troubled to listen to the sermon, and we hastened to forget the text. 'The Memoirs of Barry Lyndon' contains all these moral sentiments, yet we not only listen to them with eagerness, but they impress themselves on the mind.   In 'Catherine' and 'The Amours of Mr. Deuceace,' he had preached to unheeding ears that there were wicked people in the world, and that it behoved us to beware of them ;—we at once acknowledge that Redmond Barry is a bad man, because we recognize that he is human. Four years before, Thackeray had shouted from the housetops that it was the height of morality to talk about rascals, and here certainly we have rascality enough and to spare.   But he has completely unlearned the undefensible part of his lesson, and in giving to Redmond Barry a medley of qualities, good as well as bad, though no doubt a preponderating quality of evil, he has adopted the very method which, with un-critical haste, he had fastened on as the fault of Ainsworth and Lytton.   But no work was ever more unlike ' Jack Sheppard ' and ' Dick Turpin,' because from the real faults of these novels, from their over-colouring and want of proportion, he was preserved by a kind of artistic intuition.

Many of the characters in ' The Memoirs of Barry Lyndon' had been seen before, and all its component parts, to the student of Thackeray, were tolerably familiar, but he had never given more than a foretaste of its match-

less composition.   Yet great as the book is, and
with all its merits, it takes rank rather as a
tour de force than as a work of the highest order.
And to see that this is so, it is only necessary to
glance for a moment at things not comparable
indeed, but in this connection instructive, at
three or four of the best works of imagination.
Arthur Dimmesdale, in 'The Scarlet Letter,'
is faulty and weak, but though he has allowed
another to suffer for him, he remains capable of
an act of heroic self-sacrifice.   Miriam, in 'The
Marble Faun,' gives way to gusts of passion, but
who does not appreciate the greatness of her
character and the warmth of her heart ?   Even
Tom Jones, pleasure-loving and careless as he is,
keeps bright the pure image of Sophia.   And
these are only the central, and in two cases the
tragic characters of the books which they adorn.
What a host of others there is, who have not an
evil thought, and never did anything but a good
action.   For any people at all resembling Hilda,
or the kind Squire Allworthy, we might search
'The Memoirs of Barry Lyndon' in vain.   Indeed it may be conscientiously said, that there
is not a good man or a good woman to be found
in its pages.   There are some characters, it is

true, that are not utterly wicked, but there is none in whom vice does not immensely predominate over virtue. It would be a poor standard to set up for the masterpieces of our language to say that it was enough that vice should be charitably treated. But if that were the standard, 'The Memoirs of Barry Lyndon' would be something more than a remarkable achievement, and Thackeray would have had to wait no longer before being hailed as a classic.

From the first page to the last, the book sparkles with vivacity, and it was a stroke of genius which induced its author to allow the reckless hero to tell his own story,—a hazardous experiment always from the difficulty of the task, but in this instance crowned with complete success. It is the use of this artifice which makes the novel, though in many ways comparable with, in many ways so immeasurably the superior of 'Jonathan Wild.' It might indeed almost be laid down as an axiom, that a good man should never write an autobiography, and that a bad one should himself tell his own reminiscences. A virtuous man who recounts his own virtues can hardly escape the charges of vain-glory and self-satisfaction, and a writer

who respects the opinion of the public must,
of necessity, in following the career of a scamp,
reprehend the course of conduct which is pur-
sued. This is why Colonel Esmond, though
admirable, does not take captive our admiration,
and why Fielding, though a perfect master of
irony, has in 'Jonathan Wild' many sketches
of ironical narrative that are a little too obvious
and thin. 'Jonathan Wild' has some ad-
vantages over 'The Memoirs of Barry Lyndon.'
It contains the character of Heartfree, whose
honesty, though a little stagey, forms an excellent foil to the excesses of the hero of the
book, and there are passages in it of a humour
so broad, so Rabelaisian in their grasp, as to
be quite beyond anything of the kind that
Thackeray ever attempted. But 'The Memoirs
of Barry Lyndon' possesses a *naïveté* far more
surprising, as when we find Mr. Barry repri-
manding, with an imperturbable seriousness,
the very faults in others which he has just been
committing ; and the tenderness of the blubber-
ing scoundrel has in it something quite essentially modern. This is how he writes of the fatal
accident to his son, to whom he had guaranteed
a "good flogging" if he mounted an unbroken

pony, which when trained he had intended to give him :—"I took a great horse-whip and galloped after him in a rage, swearing I would keep my promise. But heaven forgive me! I little thought of it, when at three miles from home I met a sad procession coming towards me: peasants moaning and howling as our Irish do, the black horse led by the hand, and, on a door that some of the folks carried, my poor dear, dear little boy. There he lay in his little boots and spurs, and his little coat of scarlet and gold. His dear face was quite white, and he smiled as he held a hand out to me, and said, painfully, 'You won't whip me, will you, papa?' I could only burst into tears in reply. I have seen many and many a man dying, and there's a look about the eyes which you cannot mistake. There was a little drummer-boy I was fond of who was hit down before my company at Kühnersdorf; when I ran up to offer him some water, he looked exactly like my dear Bryan then did—there's no mistaking that awful look of the eyes."

The child is taken home, and lies in a helpless condition for two days :—"During this time the dear angel's temper seemed quite to change :

he asked his mother and me pardon for any
act of disobedience he had been guilty of
towards us ; he said often he should like to
see his brother Bullingdon. 'Bully was better
than you, papa,' he said ; 'he used not to swear
so, and he told and taught me many good things
while you were away.' And, taking a hand of
his mother and mine in each of his little clammy
ones, he begged us not to quarrel so, but love
each other, so that we might meet again in
heaven, where Bully told him quarrelsome
people never went. His mother was very much
affected by these admonitions from the poor
suffering angel's mouth ; and I was so too. I
wish she had enabled me to keep the counsel
which the dying boy gave us."

How admirably the whole thing is done : the
man's tears for the loss of his offspring, his
last hope in life, as he sadly and beautifully
calls him ; and with what truth he is made to
dash the tears away, and turn round with a
snarl on poor Lady Lyndon. Thackeray was
too well acquainted with the nature of such
men,—and there are many of them, though few
so bad as Redmond Barry,—not to know that
the last thing that the tragedy of their lives

would induce them to confess to, is a feeling of remorse.

The two next years were, it is not remarkable to find, somewhat barren in matters of production. The 'Legend of the Rhine,' a burlesque of the historical romance, is little more than a first study for 'Rebecca and Rowena,' and is too long to be as effective as the better-known parodies collected under the title of 'Punch's Prize Novelists.' The 'Journey from Cornhill to Grand Cairo' is more readable than 'The Irish Sketch-Book,' from the greater variety of the objects which are described, but the author is not so much at home as he was in Dublin or Limerick, and some of the remarks upon scenes which usually call up historical associations are bald and jejune. The splendour of Versailles irritated him, and he is annoyed with the seraglio because it is not magnificent enough. He has nothing more to say of the Pyramids than that they are surrounded by a crowd of dirty ruffians, and when the Sultan passes he tries to comfort himself by reflecting that he must be nearly the most miserable of men. In short, he finds a cause of quarrel with everything that could by any possibility awaken the sentiment of awe, or dazzle the imagination. This was, however, his practice; but so blinded is he by annoyance, that when other people take to pointing his moral, he does not stop to perceive it. "What a chivalrous absurdity," he writes, "is the banner of some high and mighty prince, hanging over his stall in Windsor Chapel, when you think of the purpose for which men are supposed to assemble there! The Church of the Knights of St. John is paved over with sprawling heraldic devices of the dead gentlemen of the dead order; as if in the next world they expected to take rank in uniformity with their pedigrees, and would be marshalled into heaven according to the orders of precedence." The heraldic devices are there for no such purpose. They are there partly to preserve the memory of the dead, as old Mortality re-cut the names on the tombstones of people of lower rank, and partly to point, as they do very effectively, the mutability of human affairs. As to the flags in St. George's Chapel, they are there not only to mark in a more artistic manner than letters can do the seats of the separate knights, but also as a visible sign, that there prince and peasant alike acknowledge a majesty before which all distinctions are forgotten.

In a later page, Thackeray gives a very fair sample of one of the ways of looking at life that were to become so familiar in 'The Book of Snobs' and its attendant productions. He is describing the tumble-down condition of sleepy old Rhodes. "A ragged squad of Turkish soldiers lolled about the gate; a couple of boys on a donkey; a grinning slave on a mule; a pair of women flapping along in yellow papooshes; a basket-maker sitting under an antique carved portal, and chanting or howling as he plaited his osiers; a peaceful well of water, at which knights' chargers had drunk, and at which the double-boyed donkey was now refreshing himself— would have made a pretty picture for a sentimental artist. As he sits and endeavours to make a sketch of this plaintive little comedy, a shabby dignitary of the island comes clatteringly by on a thirty-shilling horse, and two or three of the ragged soldiers leave their pipes to salute him as he passes under the Gothic archway." The peculiarity of the passage lies in the fact that he mentions the probable value of the horse, when any other adjective would have done as

well as the adjective of price. Had he substi-
tuted some such expression as 'a broken-down
horse,' the romance of the delicate piece of
description would have been preserved, and a
writer who falls into traps of this kind with
facility must have a more than ordinarily keen
eye for the commercial aspect of things. But
money and its influence upon society was a
subject that always had a strange fascination for
Thackeray, though never a stronger one than in
the years from 1846 to 1848.

The whole plot of the farcical story of Mr.
Jeames de la Pluche turns upon the sudden ac-
quisition of a fortune by a footman in love with
a housemaid. Of the vulgarity of newly-acquired
wealth Thackeray was no doubt cognisant, but
it was not till 'Vanity Fair' that he treated it
with the scorn that it deserves. In Mr. Jeames
it receives very gentle treatment, and the satire,
which throughout the book is never unkindly,
only begins to lose its suavity when he comes to
write of a genteel poverty that insists upon pre-
serving appearances. " Old Lord Bareacres," he
tells us, " was as stiff as a poker, as proud as
Lucifer, and as poor as Job." The sting of the
sentence is in its conclusion, and once we are

informed that he is not only indigent, but bravely determined not to confess it, we must have little knowledge of Thackeray if we expect Lord Bareacres to find any mercy at his hands. He positively delights in rendering the character contemptible, and it is but fair to say that, using all the license of burlesque, he speedily completes his intention. This is a method of enlisting the reader's sympathy in favour of one's prejudices, which a writer of fiction finds excessively convenient. If he dislikes the notion of kingship, it is as good as an argument to set Richard I. about the murder of a child.[1] If he has no high opinion of journalists, it is easy to have them at a disadvantage by locating them in the Fleet.[2] But it is a method which an essayist is debarred from employing, and when a writer is about to give rein to every one of his prejudices, essays or papers are quite the unsafest material in which to embody them.

It was, therefore, by an artistic mistake so serious as to be remarkable in the author of 'Barry Lyndon,' that Thackeray was induced to put his reflections upon English society into the

[1] 'Rebecca and Rowena.'
[2] Captain Shandon in 'Pendennis.'

form of 'The Book of Snobs.' 'The Book of Snobs' is only not a failure, because every now and then it is enlivened with anecdotes, and far the most readable part of it is the comparatively lengthy history of Major and Mrs. Ponto. It is not long before the reader is completely weary of the discursive series of papers, and it is difficult to believe that they were much less tiresome as they came out week by week in the pages of 'Punch.' It is not merely that there are too many of them ; they have little or no connection with each other, and, as Mr. Trollope has pointed out, the word snob is made to embrace so much, that it loses its precision and interest. It is impossible, it seems, to avoid being a snob, unless one dines upon chops and porter, and marries on nothing a year. But though it is not clear from the book what is a snob, or rather what a snob is not, an instructive catalogue of what was obnoxious to Thackeray could readily be compiled from it.

He applies the term snob indiscriminately to every person he dislikes, and for this purpose he sweeps together James I., Louis XIV., and the Prince Consort, though there is no other likeness between them than that they were royal ; but

F

Thackeray hated the ceremonial of courts. He so despised all forms of pretentiousness that he would have erected a universal palace of truth. If he had had his will, old women would have gone about bald-headed, and his Lady Susan Scrapers would have proclaimed their monetary difficulties aloud. Though there is nothing to be ashamed of in poverty, people may be pardoned for struggling against a reversal of fortune, and the satirist who thought it was a disgrace that at the Universities rich and poor should be distinguished by their costume, might have had some sympathy with a gentlewoman who, when she lost money, did not at once diminish her state.

There are many passages, no doubt, in 'The Book of Snobs,' in which the little meannesses of men are ridiculed with temperance and justice, but the whole philosophy of it is wrong. "He who meanly admires mean things," says Thackeray, "is a snob," but that is not how he used the word, nor what it is generally supposed to connote. A snob neither admires mean, nor despises great things. He admires and despises the things which he ought to admire and despise, but he admires overmuch,

and despises without a sense of proportion. It
is not in his admiration or contempt, but in
their quality, that he is in error, and it would be
much more near the truth to say, if the phrase
were read with proper limitations, that a snob is
one who wrongly admires the right things. But
it is not easy to define a snob, as the word has
acquired an artificially restricted meaning ; and
it is obvious that a man might wrongly admire
the right things without being snobbish, as the
mistaken admiration might arise from ignorance
and not from snobbery. A man might con-
ceivably admire the Madonna di San Sisto, not
on account of its own excellence, but because it
reminded him of a much inferior painting. But
though this is true, and though it is evident that
the class that wrongly admires is wider than the
" genus snob," the characteristic of the genus, in
so far as it has a characteristic, is an undue and
false admiration of certain things quite admirable in themselves. These things, as the word
snob is now used, will all be found to be connected in some way or another with the ideas
of rank, wealth, dignity, or power. To be mistaken in one's admiration for this restricted
class of objects is to run in danger of snobbery,

but to safeguard oneself by refusing to admire
them at all is to make a graver mistake. There
is nothing mean in those ideas, on the contrary,
they are the antithesis of what is mean ; and to
say that it is snobbish to meanly admire mean
things is to shoot very wide of the mark. In
this epigram, which depends on an adverb and
an adjective, the adverb hardly conveys the
right idea, and the epithet is exactly wrong.
Rank and wealth have had privileges extended
to them in all countries and at all times, and
unless the government of mankind has been
conducted from the beginning on false prin-
ciples, they are no more mean, and they have
as much right to evoke their proper share of
admiration, as learning, or courage, or any other
of those abstract ideas which command habitual
respect. "The word snob," writes M. Taine,
"does not exist in France, because they have
not the thing." This is not the reason of the
poverty of the French language in this particular.
Wherever there are distinctions of place or
wealth, and quite irrespective of the form of
government, there will be found many to over-
estimate their value.

To take only two instances :—The same

feeling that, in unworthy excess, prompts a man to be ashamed of being a *novus homo*, is responsible for the motto " Noblesse oblige," and has made government by oligarchies historically possible. The same feeling, that, disproportioned and absurd, induces us to think poverty dishonourable, awakens us to a sense of the value of those privileges of environment and education, which only money has the power to confer. Snobbery, indeed, is a much more complex and a much less humorous affair than Thackeray imagined, and the sudden changes of fortune in families and individuals may be looked at as well from their serious as from their ridiculous side. It is no unusual thing for a man to raise himself in the world, and to become fitted to take his place in a different society from that of his origin. Let him formerly have been a footman, and if he is momentarily flustered at the ill-timed arrival of the washerwoman and the coalheaver, many of the readers of novels will be content to laugh,[1] and to label him a snob ; but let him be Carlyle writing to his future wife that her mother

---

[1] 'The Diary of C. Jeames de la Pluche.'

and his must not meet,[1] and the sentiment
aroused is more akin to tears than to mirth.
The critical intelligence of the public has not
been slow to seize upon this, and to resent the
one-sided aspect from which Thackeray viewed,
and the liberty with which he treated, failings
that have their root in the necessary conditions
of life.   And indeed there is something harsh
and uncharitable in a book that has nothing
else to say of pride, shame, and ambition, but
that they are all forms, more or less disguised,
of a snobbery that is rampant everywhere.   The
critic would have cause for anger in the flip-
pancy of the attitude, even were the remarks,
with this deduction, otherwise fair ; but when
he finds their author gravely telling him, that
from the institution of civil society, man has felt
pride and shame on the wrong occasions, and
that the objects of his ambition have always
been misplaced, patience is exhausted, and ' The
Book of Snobs ' is speedily condemned.

Once started, however, on an investigation
into the faults and foibles of contemporary
existence, Thackeray was not a writer to re-

[1] ' Thomas Carlyle,' by John Nichol.   English Men of
Letters Series, p. 47.

linquish it until he had exhausted his invention,
and pointed the same moral in a hundred similar
ways. 'Mrs. Perkins's Ball,' 'Our Street,' and
'A Little Dinner at Timmins's' quickly followed
each other from the press, and in them the
satirist has the immense advantage of being
able to make the fictitious snobs whom he
assembles together as ridiculous as his fancy
desires. They are all nearly entirely narrative,
and the author seldom ventures on a reflection ;
if he does, he is betrayed into his earlier manner.
He has been describing a young man of fashion
" who would borrow ten guineas from any man
in the room, in the most jovial way possible,"
and he adds,—" When I see these magnificent
dandies yawning out of ' White's ' or caracoling
in the Park on shining chargers, I like to think
that Brummel was the greatest of them all, and
that Brummel's father was a footman." The
habits of fops are contemptible, because they
can be learnt in a generation. How much better
is Horace's simple chronicle of his desires and
tastes,—" Persicos odi, puer, apparatus."

In 'Mrs. Perkins's Ball' and 'Our Street,' the
names of the guests, and the headings of the
chapters, are a fair index to their style. There

is Mrs. Perkins, who entertains beyond her
means ; Mr. Minchin, a simpering barrister ;
Mr. Flam, a flatterer; Miss Meggot, a neglected
spinster ; Mr. Winter, a satirist; Miss Toady ;
and the Lords Methuselah, Billygoat, and Tar-
quin : while in 'Our Street' we have such titles
as " The Bungalow," " Captain and Mrs. Bragg,"
" Levant House Chambers," " Some of the
Servants," " The Dove of the Street," " The
Bumpshers," and " Somebody whom nobody
knows."

In 'A Little Dinner at Timmins's,' Thackeray,
to render the account more graphic, condescended
to allow the story of their " somewhat osten-
tatious hospitality " to be told by one who had
partaken of the feast.   So anxious was he to
hunt down this particular form of what he called
snobbery, that to effect his purpose he was ready
to act in a manner which he had been the first
to deride.[1]   The ' Little Sketches and Travels
in London' are marred by no fault of this sort,
and no better idea could be given of the range
of Thackeray's intellect than by comparing them

[1] Cf. the comment on Lord L.'s travels in 'The Book
of Snobs' (chapter iii., Influence of the Aristocracy on
Snobs).

with 'The Book of Snobs' and 'Mrs. Perkins's
Ball.' A man of no great diversity of mind
may, at different times, look at the same subject
from different points of view ; but it is in the
insensible gradations of one particular mood, so
difficult to seize upon, and so obvious at once,
that the capacity of a really fertile and various
writer is most conclusively shown. The 'Travels
in London' point much the same moral as the
other books of this period, and they are likewise
occupied in satirizing those who pay undue
attention to trifles, but the gentle if slightly
senile benignity that breathes in their pages
gives us a regard for their author, and there are
few who have not a warm place somewhere in
their hearts for Don Pacifico and Spec.

CHAPTER II

ON the threshold of 'Vanity Fair' the attention of the student is arrested by a work not so remarkable in itself as in its subject and the time selected for its publication. It is a collection of parodies, and bore the title of 'Punch's Prize Novelists.' These sketches have received all the praise which it is possible to bestow on this species of composition. They have been called the best of parodies, and where there were no serious competitors it was easy for a man of Thackeray's eminence to distance what competition there was, but they appeared simultaneously with the production of his own bid for success. They are characterized by little of the rudeness of the earlier 'Epistle to the Literati,' but he was engaged in satirizing his great contemporaries at the moment when he was clamouring to be admitted of their company. Mr. Arnold combined the functions of poet and critic, and a serious estimate of Tennyson or Browning would have been welcome from his pen, but he never could be induced to refer, except in the conventional language of compliment, to any original writer of his time. This was, perhaps, to err on the other side; but Byron's references to "Wordsworth, Coleridge, Southey," and Shelley's 'Peter Bell the Third,' are blots upon their fame. The one, however, was but an occasional burst of irritation, the other a solitary lapse. But that Thackeray should sit down whenever he was tired of 'Vanity Fair,' to laugh at the other travellers who had brought back different accounts of that city, forms an instructive commentary on his character.

Of the many-sidedness and perplexity of that character there was further proof to come, but 'Vanity Fair' itself gave no added demonstration of it. The book is singularly straightforward. The same attitude is preserved throughout, and that attitude, though severer than, is in all essentials similar to that formerly adopted. There is a greater diversity in the personages of the novel, and more sagacity in the commentary which accompanies the record of their doings than is to be found in any of Thackeray's earlier works. But the figures are such as we should have expected him, when concentrating his faculties, to be able to draw, and the sentiments have nothing surprising in them, coming from the author of ' Catherine,' ' The Hoggarty Diamond,' and ' The Book of Snobs.' Miss Wirt, the governess of the two Miss Osbornes, was formerly in the service of Major Ponto ; Dobbin's fight at Slaughter House School is a repetition of Mr. Frank Berry's ; Deuceace, Viscount Cinqbars, and Lord Bareacres flit about in the background, and just as the mother of the heroine of ' The Ravenswing ' was a ballet-dancer, so Mrs. Sharp is an opera-girl. These are not merely superficial resemblances, but there are others that are still more striking. " The richly - dressed figure of the wicked nobleman " is merely a compound of all those vices which Thackeray had for long pointed out as appertaining especially to the aristocracy. Dennis Haggarty's devotion to a woman unworthy of him gave a hint for Dobbin's ; Rawdon Crawley has not the ability of Redmond Barry or of Deuceace, but he has as many of

their vices as were compatible with his stupidity ;
Amelia gave scope for an elaborate study of
the virtues of Mary Titmarsh and Caroline
Gann ; while it is easy to see that Becky is a
cleverer Catherine Hayes, moving in a higher
rank of society, and amid less melodramatic
surroundings. Mr. Sedley in his misfortunes,
and Mr. Osborne in his prosperity, are both
indebted to the earlier portraiture of the oil-
merchant in 'A Shabby Genteel Story'; the
feelings entertained for Caroline by the Misses
Macarthy, and those that characterize the relations of George Osborne's sisters with his
fiancée, are the same with a difference ; while
Sir Pitt has as much bluster as Sir George
Tufto, and more vulgar arrogance than Lord
Crabs.

The origins of George Osborne, Pitt Crawley,
and Miss Briggs, it is true, are not so easily
traceable ; and though Miss Hoggarty's money
had been an object of much solicitude to Mr.
Brough, she has no other likeness to Miss
Crawley. Major O'Dowd and his wife, and the
admirably drawn Jos Sedley, are also original.
But though these figures give variety to the
canvas, and we are forced to confess that we

do not recognize them, they all have a family likeness to the people whom we already knew, and take their places naturally by their sides. Nor is the treatment accorded to these characters unfamiliar. The sub-title of the book is 'A Novel without a Hero,' a phrase that, effective as it is, fails to express the meaning of the author. There was nothing to necessitate a flourish in the absence of a hero. Shakespeare wrote plays without a hero :—the interest of one is centred in Lady Macbeth, and in 'Twelfth Night' it is Olivia and Viola who arrest our attention ; while 'The Blithedale Romance' subordinates Miles Coverdale and Hollingsworth to the more commanding personality of Zenobia. Rebecca Sharp takes up as much of the space of 'Vanity Fair' as is usually allocated to a heroine, and there was nothing remarkable in giving to a woman the chief position in a tale. The characteristic of 'Vanity Fair' is not that it has no hero, but that there is nothing heroic in it, and this it is that differentiates the novel from the works of other writers, and supplies the real reason of its effect upon the public. But this, for Thackeray, was not a new departure ; on the contrary, it is this that furnishes the

distinct peculiarity of all his earlier tales.
'Vanity Fair' came with the novelty of a new
sensation, only because they were so little read.
But the book itself is the best justification of its
success.

In some ways it is the most striking thing
that Thackeray ever did. He never surpassed
it for quiet observation of character, and for the
skill with which he has contrived to make the
most unreal and fantastic of its personages
appear to live. But it is hard, one-sided, and
the peculiarity which made it famous is the most
marked of its defects. It has been said that it
is an actual transcript from life, but the 'Mid-
summer Night's Dream' is more near to reality.
While we read the book, so great is its fascination, we can almost believe it to be true, but
as soon as we lay it down, the narrative begins
to assume its true form for us, and we see it as
it is, from the beginning to the end " one entire
impossibility." It is not that the characters are
impossible, though some of them are impossible
enough. It is not that no woman was ever
simply a calculating machine, it is not that no
man was ever merely sanctimonious, it is not
that no baronet was ever a brutal bully and

nothing more, or a peer ever wholly profligate, or a merchant ever made up only of vulgarity and rage, because such people have on rare occasions existed, and may by possibility again. It is not in this that the impossibility consists, but such a collection was never got together in one corner of the world. There are two good people in the book,—Dobbin, who is a simpleton, and Amelia, who is a fool. But these are not the only virtuous inhabitants of the Vanity Fair in which we live. If it were otherwise, if there were no other virtuous inhabitants, a man walking through it would not only "not be oppressed by his own or other people's hilarity," but he would decline, and very properly decline, to walk through it at all. If life were as Thackeray depicts it in 'Vanity Fair,' not only would the earth be more sparsely populated than it is, but it would have been impossible for true virtue ever to have manifested itself. Virtue being the product of precept and example, Scott could not have lived, nor the qualities of the Vicar of Wakefield had opportunity to develop. Had the world been peopled with Neros, there would have been no room for Seneca, and were every one a Crawley or a Sharp, Esmond's self-sacrifice or Colonel Newcome's heroism would never have been understood.

In 'The Memoirs of Barry Lyndon' the company is worse than in 'Vanity Fair,' and 'The Memoirs of Barry Lyndon' is a triumph of art but it would have been far from a triumph if we had been asked to take the company there assembled as a fair representation of society. We should have rejected it at once as an imposture, whereas the falsehood underlying 'Vanity Fair' is only apparent—and it is a tribute to Thackeray's power—after a careful perusal of the work. But when this fact is allowed, when we turn to look at 'Vanity Fair' not as a portrait, not even as a caricature of society, but as a brilliant painting of a section of it, there remains much that is admirable. It is almost as difficult to draw a woman without a heart as a woman without a soul, and the latter has not yet been seriously attempted. Mr. Benson's Dodo is an ingenious and clever study of such a character, but it is only necessary to compare his method with Thackeray's to see why he has failed, and how much he has under-rated the gravity of the task. Thackeray devotes all his resources to the creation of Becky Sharp.

G

He was well aware how long a course of observation had to be undertaken before even the broad lines of such a figure could be accurately sketched. And it is this that makes him watch Becky with a solicitude that might deceive the reader into imagining that her creator could not resist occasionally admiring her cleverness and resource. He calls her " darling," it is true ; but the epithet is always abusive, never laudatory, and though in a sense she is the darling of his eye, it is only that he knew that, if he was for a moment to lose sight of her, her interest for the reader could not have been sustained. She is hardly ever absent from the stage, and her introduction is so bold that Mr. Trollope thought it must have slipped in by mistake. " No school-girl," he writes, " who ever lived would have thrown back her gift-book as Rebecca did the 'dixonary' out of the carriage-window as she was taken away from school." The error is comprehensible, even in so acute a critic, but the facts are quite the other way. No woman so selfish and calculating as Becky afterwards became could have failed to make mistakes of temper and forwardness in her youth. It was natural that she should speak French to Miss

Pinkerton, who could not understand it, and bestow on Jos Sedley " ever so gentle a pressure with her hand." " The latter," says Thackeray, " was an advance, and as such, perhaps, some ladies of indisputable correctness and gentility will condemn the action as immodest ; but, you see, poor dear Rebecca had all this work to do for herself. If a person is too poor to keep a servant, though ever so elegant, he must sweep his own rooms ; if a dear girl has no dear Mamma to settle with the young man, she must do it for herself." And it was equally natural that when elated by her marriage with the son of a baronet, she should forget her manners, and speak rudely to George Osborne. " What an honour," she says to him, " to have had you for a brother-in-law, you are thinking ? To be sister-in-law to George Osborne, Esquire, son of John Osborne, Esquire, son of—what was your grandpapa, Mr. Osborne ? "

Her second appearance as Clytemnestra is, however, less to be defended. She had by that time acquired too much experience to risk, even when driven to bay, poisoning Jos Sedley ; but the incident is improbable, not impossible, and the same artist who leaves a lingering suspicion that Lord Steyne may, at the last moment, have been baulked of his prey, refrains from deliberately accusing her of murder. The introduction of Sir Pitt Crawley, on the other hand, is caricature, and Mr. Trollope is justified in supposing that it must have been written before any of the other members of the Crawley family had been conceived. And what a family it is ; a selfish old woman who has money, a dissolute clergyman, a hypocritical diplomatist, and a dissipated bully. But they all manage to preserve some relation to humanity, and their actions and sentiments are for the most part chronicled with a strange fidelity to life.

"'Shut up your sarmons, Pitt, when Miss Crawley comes down,' said his father. 'She has written to say that she won't stand the preachifying.'

"'O sir, consider the servants.'

"'The servants be hanged,' said Sir Pitt ; and his son thought even worse would happen were they deprived of the benefit of his instruction.

"'Why, hang it, Pitt !' said the father to his remonstrance, 'you wouldn't be such a flat as to let three thousand a year go out of the family.'

"'What is money compared to our souls, sir?' continued Mr. Crawley.

"'You mean that the old lady won't leave the money to you?' And who knows but it was Mr. Crawley's meaning."

For Rawdon Crawley it is difficult to understand Thackeray's admiration. He calls him " honest Rawdon," with real fondness in his voice, and seems to pity him for his connection with his wife. But the man was a drunkard and a cheat long before Becky had anything to do with him ; and we are left to supply the occasion of the duel which ended disastrously for Captain Marker. Duelling days were nearly over then, and it is as likely as not that Captain Marker had some serious cause for offence. That Rawdon should experience a passion for a fascinating governess was nothing particularly meritorious. He did not expect to lose money by it, and when he discovered that he had, even he had sense enough to perceive that he owed something to the woman who alone was able to keep him above water. Besides, the money was never really his, and he was too stupid to appreciate the excellence of his chance. That he should beat an old man who had been intriguing with his wife so openly that every one but he had seen it long before, was no more praise-worthy than the resentment of a thief when his own property is stolen. It is true that there was a pitch of baseness to which he could not bring himself to descend, and he returned the price of Becky's dishonour to Lord Steyne ; but he sulkily accepted from the same noble-man the considerable income of a sinecure which he could easily have refused, and for the slight duties of which he was totally unfit. All this was natural enough, but it was no subject for admiration ; and though it was human of him to be fond of his son, there was as much merit in the maudlin tears of Redmond Barry, or the pleasure Catherine took in the fine clothes of the adopted son of Mr. Hayes.

It is one thing to treat vice with charity, and quite another to speak of its professors with affection. The same book that spoke of " honest Rawdon " could hardly contain a character that would ensure our respect. Amelia fails even to enlist our sympathy. In prosperity she is childish, in adversity she becomes petted and wilful, and Mr. Senior has pointed out that her reluctance to part with her boy is due wholly to a desire that they should not be separated, not to any fear of the prejudicial results for him that might arise from acquaintance with the Osbornes. She is passionately devoted during his life to George Osborne, who half despises her, and after his death she cherishes a romantic attachment to his memory. To Amelia Sedley, however, a large portion of the book is devoted, and it is not to be supposed that she should not occasionally be betrayed into animation. Thackeray's purpose in delineating this character was twofold ; he introduced her first as an example of the negative virtues, and afterwards continued the study of her disposition as a foil to that of Becky. He maintains an unswerving determination to keep her as we first met her, a timid, expansive school-girl, with a fund of maudlin sensibility dangerously apt to develop into selfishness. Again and again, in her passages with Dobbin, Thackeray resists the temptation to endow her with a heart, and where one would have expected from the most long-suffering, righteous anger, or an outburst of wronged and passionate love, we find only sobs and protestations, and a page of sentimental reflection. Once or twice she finds her lot too hard, and becomes peevishly unreasonable, as in the scene with Mrs. Sedley and the baby's medicine, or flings out into a momentary burst of irritation. But these passages are for the most part calculated, and have a touch of artifice. They serve to vary the monotony of her characterless virtue, but they give a laboured effect to the portrait. Once only Nature takes the pen from his hand, and allows us to have a peep at the heart of this too real Cinderella. It is the morning after the Duchess of Richmond's ball, when the English officers have left for Waterloo. At the ball Becky (Mrs. Crawley) has concluded her long and successful siege of Amelia's husband, Captain Osborne. Mrs. Crawley bears the absence of " honest Rawdon " lightly, and calls upon Amelia to condole with her on her anxiety :—

" After the first movement of terror in Amelia's mind—when Rebecca's green eyes lighted upon her, and rustling in her fresh silks and brilliant ornaments, the latter tripped up with extended arms to embrace her—a feeling of anger succeeded, and from being deadly pale before, her face flushed up red, and she returned Rebecca's look after a moment with a steadiness which surprised and somewhat abashed her rival.

"'Dearest Amelia, you are very unwell,' the visitor said, putting forth her hand to take Amelia's. 'What is it? I could not rest until I knew how you were.'

"Amelia drew back her hand—never since her life began had that gentle soul refused to believe or to answer any demonstration of goodwill or affection. But she drew back her hand and trembled all over. 'Why are *you* here, Rebecca?' she said, still looking at her solemnly with her large eyes. These glances troubled her visitor.

"'She must have seen him give me the letter at the ball,' ·Rebecca thought. 'Don't be agitated, dear Amelia,' she said, looking down. 'I came but to see if I could—if you were well.'

"'Are you well?' said Amelia. 'I dare say you are. You don't love your husband. You would not be here if you did. Tell me, Rebecca, did I ever do you anything but kindness?'

"'Indeed, Amelia, no,' the other said, still hanging down her head.

"'When you were quite poor, who was it that befriended you? Was I not a sister to you? You saw us all in happier days before he married me. I was all in all then to him; or would he have given up his fortune, his family, as he nobly did to make me happy? Why did you come between my love and me? Who sent you to separate those whom God joined, and take my darling's heart from me—my own husband? Do you think you could love him as I did? His love was everything to me. You knew it, and wanted to rob me of it. For shame, Rebecca; bad and wicked woman—false friend and false wife.'

"'Amelia, I protest before God, I have done my husband no wrong,' Rebecca said, turning from her.

"'Have you done *me* no wrong, Rebecca? You did not succeed, but you tried. Ask your heart if you did not?'

" She knows nothing, Rebecca thought.

"'He came back to me. I knew he would. I knew that no falsehood, no flattery, could keep him from me long. I knew he would come. I prayed so that he should.'

" The poor girl spoke these words with a spirit

and volubility which Rebecca had never before seen in her, and before which the latter was quite dumb. 'But what have I done to you,' she continued in a more pitiful tone, 'that you should try and take him from me ? I had him but for six weeks. You might have spared me those, Rebecca. And yet, from the very first day of our wedding, you came and blighted it. Now he is gone, are you come to see how unhappy I am ?' she continued. 'You made me wretched enough for the past fortnight : you might have spared me to-day.'

"'I—I never came here,' interposed Rebecca, with unlucky truth.

"'No. You didn't come. You took him away. Are you come to fetch him from me ? ' she continued in a wilder tone. 'He was here, but he is gone now. There on that very sofa he sate. Don't touch it. We sate and talked there. I was on his knee, and my arms were round his neck, and we said "Our Father." Yes, he was here : and they came and took him away, but he promised me to come back.'

"'He will come back, my dear,' said Rebecca, touched in spite of herself.

"'Look,' said Amelia, 'this is his sash—isn't

it a pretty colour?' and she took up the fringe
and kissed it. She had tied it round her waist
at some part of the day. She had forgotten her
anger, her jealousy, the very presence of her
rival seemingly. For she walked silently, and
almost with a smile on her face, towards the
bed, and began to smooth down George's
pillow.

"Rebecca walked, too, silently away. 'How
is Amelia?' asked Jos, who still held his position
in the chair.

"'There should be somebody with her,' said
Rebecca. 'I think she is very unwell': and she
went away with a very grave face, refusing Mr.
Sedley's entreaties that she would stay and
partake of the early dinner which he had
ordered."

But Amelia never again rises to this height of
womanly indignation, and she sinks back into
the spiritless creature whom the worthy and
clumsy Dobbin was content to pursue. His
devotion is disinterested and noble, but it is
expended on so poor an object that it lessens
him in our esteem. She was no "dear lady
Disdain," whose waywardness increased her
attraction, and it is natural and fitting that her

knight-errant should be as uninteresting as herself.

Thackeray might have gauged the effect Amelia would have upon the public from the fate he prescribes for Dobbin. Like her, he is a compound of all the negative virtues, though he has a warmer heart, and is, as all soldier-heroes, necessarily courageous. But she prefers the memory of her first husband, who, if he had few virtues, had just enough character to commit occasional and ineffectual sins. His approbation was perhaps also the more precious as she was conscious of having partially lost it. As to Dobbin's affection, it was to be had long before it was asked, and always at her command. He is so formally precise that he cannot even blunder into his own happiness, and it is by a subtle touch of irony that he is made to win Amelia at length, not because her sentiments towards him are altered, but because she has discovered that her first husband was unfaithful. "This is what he has asked for every day and hour for eighteen years. This is what he pined after. Here it is—the summit, the end—the last page of the third volume." Well might Thackeray conclude his book with the melancholy

question, "Ah, Vanitas Vanitatum! which of us
has his desire? or having it is satisfied?"

A satirist speaking in this tone, and offering
at the same time to the world so extended a
gallery of portraits, was bound, however, to
secure attention, and the success of 'Vanity
Fair,' though not immediate, was very great.
But the influence of what Carlyle has called
"the poison of popular applause" is not always
beneficial, and as often as not has proved the
ruin of a writer. Those who have long listened
for it in vain are too apt to be intoxicated with
it when it comes. Thackeray had waited ten
years for it, but when it came it was of ines-
timable service to his nature. Like Byron, he
woke one morning to find himself famous, but
he also, like Rip van Winkle, awoke to discover
that he was a hundred years older than when he
fell asleep ;—so great is the gap that lies between
the sober observation and large humanity of 'Pendennis' and the brilliant satire and character-
drawing of 'Vanity Fair.' Under the rays of a
steady sun of popularity, the seeds of latent
and unsuspected qualities in him began to grow.
Once sure of his public, he far less often was
betrayed into those faults of over-statement and

exaggeration of manner with which he had caught its ear. He had played the satirist to good effect in ' Vanity Fair,' but after all it was a game ; and as much satire as was really genuine to Thackeray is to be found in ' Pendennis,' ' Esmond,' and ' The Newcomes.' Two trifles of this period serve sufficiently to mark the change. In ' Mr. Brown's Letters to his Nephew,' the garrulous old man, "full of wise saws and modern instances," has always a kind word for the follies from which he warns the younger, and a fellow-feeling for the youthful indiscretions which he knows well his correspondent will commit. In ' Dr. Birch and his young Friends ' we have the spectacle of an author, always determined to see sermons in stones, if not good in everything, coping successfully with the difficulties of an unromantic subject. Childhood is pretty when it is kept in the place of childhood, and bears its proper relation to age. There is no lovelier couple than a mother and a child, nothing pleasanter to contemplate than a father's love for his boy. But when children are placed in unnatural situations, they lose all the qualities which induce us to care for them. A boarding-school, however useful for hardening the character, in an age when most have to "fend for themselves," contains of necessity conditions that are quite out of the course of nature. It is there that we see youths with all the exaggerated sense of individuality characteristic of the beginning period of life, aping the conduct, and assuming the attitudes, of middle-aged men. As a result we have there independence without restraint, and selfishness unrelieved by any knowledge of our comparative unimportance to others.

Boys, moreover, however high an opinion they may have of themselves, are seldom remarkable for self-respect, and they will pay a far higher price than grown-up people for immunity from ill-usage, and for their own personal security. To ingratiate themselves with the powerful, the weak will take sides against the weak. Hence it is that the strong, who are not ashamed to use their strength, are always secure of a servile following, and that, at school, to be unpopular is to lose every friend. These things happen of necessity where both body and spirit are timid and unformed, but they are not pleasant to look back upon, and English authors, writing for an English public, have found them convenient to forget. For these reasons alone it would be idle to expect that an accurate or serious portrait of school-boy life should ever be drawn, but there are others equally powerful that help to obscure the past, and it is the lot of many to come to look back upon it from the troubles and distress of life as a vague but glorious period, or to suppose that the actions which they but dimly remember were prompted by the same feelings which, in similar circumstances, would have actuated them in manhood or in age. Canon Farrar's 'Eric' is the product of one of these ideas, 'Tom Brown's School-days' of the other. Eric is a sentimental impossibility, and Tom Brown is merely an average middle-aged Briton, with a better appetite, and a greater interest in football. In a field of this kind, Thackeray's triumph with his little comedy is the more unique. He glosses over nothing, and his boys are no older than their years, but the portrait drawn is not repellent, and if while reading it we regret, we also understand, the follies and the vices of our youth. He watches and comments on the little fortunes of his human

H

beings in miniature with a perception which is never at fault, and with a wisdom that is always bland.

> Come wealth or want, come good or ill,
> Let young and old accept their part,
> And bow before the awful Will,
> And bear it with an honest heart.
> Who misses, or who wins the prize ?
> Go lose or conquer as you can :
> But if you fail or if you rise,
> Be each, pray God, a gentleman.

CHAPTER III

'PENDENNIS' AND AFTER

'THE History of Pendennis,' the work that immediately succeeded 'Vanity Fair,' both from its importance and from its unlikeness to anything Thackeray had done before, demands a close inspection. In his shorter efforts, whatever we may think of them, however good or bad they individually may be, the story was always constructed with care, and led for the most part naturally enough to the conclusion. Even in 'Vanity Fair' it was essential that Becky should rise before she could fall. Her rise might have been brought about by other means, no doubt, and much of the embroidery of the novel is unnecessary to the plot. There is little that must have happened or that is inevitable in 'Vanity Fair,' but at least it has a central idea. 'Pendennis,' on the other hand, may be said with safety to have no story at all. It is so carelessly constructed that the incidents of Fanny and Miss Costigan are practically identical, and the opening scene is so abrupt that it requires, and receives, seventy pages of elucidation. 'Pendennis,' besides, is a satirical work. It is satire all through, and serious satire, and whenever before Thackeray had written satire seriously, his accent had been harsh. But it would be difficult to imagine an urbanity more undisturbed than belongs to the satirist of 'Pendennis,' and there is no kindlier combination of observation and wit in the language, than is contained in the first volume of the novel.

In his preface he sets out accurately the object of the book. " It is an attempt to describe one of the gentlemen of our age, one no better nor worse than most educated men " ; and again, " A little more frankness than is customary has been attempted in this story ; with no bad desire on the writer's part, it is hoped, and with no ill consequence to any reader. . . . Truth is best, from whatever chair." It is odd, however, to find an author so gravely unconscious of his own inconsistency. It was just two years

before that 'Vanity Fair' had been ushered
into the world as also a fair representation of
society. Two pictures so dissimilar could not
both be true, and the author of 'Pendennis,' one
would have thought, must have been alive to
the shortcomings of his earlier book. But to
make any such supposition would be to misunderstand the character of Thackeray. His
manner of writing was desultory, and he was
always ready to give rein to whatever mood was
uppermost. He rarely formed any conception
of a book before he had finished it, and never
took the trouble to think about the canons of
his art. He stumbled on right methods, just as
he floundered into mistakes. After 'Pendennis,'
he was capable of writing 'The Kickleburys on
the Rhine'; after 'Esmond,' 'The Wolves and
the Lamb'; and after 'The Newcomes,' of
serving that little drama up again in the form
of 'Lovel the Widower.' It is no matter of
surprise, therefore, that the author of 'Catherine'
should tell us in the preface to 'Pendennis' that
the manners of ruffians and gaol-birds were to
him quite unfamiliar, whereas it would be more
true to say that 'Pendennis' was his first considerable story in which there were not more

than plenty of them. The nearest approach to a ruffian in the book is John Armstrong Amory Altamont, and he, as if to make the statement in the preface good, is not merely a badly-drawn character, but goes off, like the villain in a fairy tale, in pantomimic smoke. There are other characters, however, that are by no means amiable. Sir Francis Clavering is so despicable in his weakness and wickedness, that it is only by the skill with which he is portrayed that he becomes sufficiently human to serve his purpose in the story ; and it would be hard to find anything besides her "sensibility" to recommend Blanche Amory to our affection.

But 'Pendennis' is not made up of these characters ; and from Alcide Mirobolant, the miraculous French cook, to the Prince of Fairoaks himself, from Madame Fribsby to Laura Bell, there is hardly one of them who does not say or do something for which the reader would wish to shake them by what he is fain to believe are their substantial hands. They are no compounds of vices "that come like shadows," no puppets that dance before the booths of Vanity Fair as the showman cries his sermon, but real living men and women, and nothing would surprise us less than to see Major Pendennis eyeing us from a club window as we walked down Pall Mall, or to have to listen after lunch to Lady Clavering's interminable troubles. Even the old apothecary, Arthur's father, looks out from the pages a staid and familiar little figure :—

"The old man never spoke about the shop himself, never alluded to it ; called in the medical practitioner of Clavering to attend his family ; sunk the black breeches and stockings altogether ; attended markets and sessions, and wore a bottle-green coat and brass buttons with drab gaiters, just as if he had been an English gentleman all his life. He used to stand at his lodge gate, and see the coaches come in, and bow gravely to the guards and coachmen as they touched their hats and drove by. It was he who founded the Clavering book club ; and set up the Samaritan soup and blanket society. It was he who brought the mail, which used to run through Cacklefield before, away from that village and through Clavering. At church he was equally active as a vestryman and wor- shipper. At market, every Thursday, he went from pen to stall ; looked at samples of oats and munched corn ; felt beasts, punched geese

in the breast, and weighed them with a knowing
air; and did business with the farmers of the
Clavering Arms, as well as the oldest frequenter
of that house of call. It was now his shame,
as it formerly was his pride, to be called doctor,
and those who wished to please him always
gave him the title of Squire.

"Heaven knows where they came from, but
a whole range of Pendennis portraits presently
hung round the Doctor's oak dining-room;
Lelys and Vandykes he vowed all the portraits
to be, and when questioned as to the history
of the originals, would vaguely say they were
'ancestors of his.' His little boy believed in
them to their fullest extent, and Roger Pendennis of Agincourt, Arthur Pendennis of Creçy,
General Pendennis of Blenheim and Oudenarde,
were as real and actual beings for this young
gentleman as—whom shall we say?—as Robin-
son Crusoe, or Peter Wilkins, or the Seven
Champions of Christendom, whose histories
were in his library."

This is satire certainly, but how different in
tone from the cruel comments on the shifts of
Becky, or the rough jeer that assailed the household of the Pontos. In 'Vanity Fair' the Mar-

quis of Steyne is represented without a single
virtue to balance his "thousand crimes." In
'Pendennis' Thackeray utilized his previous and
bald creation to complete a stroke of consum-
mate art. Major Pendennis, Arthur's bachelor
uncle, we learn in the novel itself, is a man of
the world whose emotions are not easily aroused.
The Marquis of Steyne those who had read
'Vanity Fair' knew to be cold and heartless to
a degree.

"The next day Major Pendennis was going
out shooting, about noon, with some of the
gentlemen staying at Lord Steyne's house ; and
the company, waiting for the carriages, were
assembled on the terrace in front of the house,
when a fly drove up from the neighbouring
station, and a grey-headed, rather shabby old
gentleman, jumped out, and asked for Major
Pendennis. It was Mr. Bows. He took the
Major aside and spoke to him; most of the
gentlemen round about saw that something
serious had happened, from the alarmed look
of the Major's face.

"Wagg said, 'It's a bailiff come down to
nab the Major'; but nobody laughed at the
pleasantry.

" ' Hullo ! What's the matter, Pendennis ? ' cried Lord Steyne, with his strident voice. ' Anything wrong ? '

" ' It's—it's—my boy that's *dead*,' said the Major, and burst into a sob—the old man was quite overcome.

" ' Not dead, my lord ; but very ill when I left London,' Mr. Bows said, in a low voice.

" A britzska came up at this moment as the three men were speaking. The Peer looked at his watch. ' You've twenty minutes to catch the mail train. Jump in, Pendennis ; and drive like h——, sir, do you hear ? '

" The carriage drove off swiftly with Pendennis and his companions, and let us trust that the oath will be pardoned to the Marquis of Steyne."

The long episode of the Costigans is told with equal truth, and in its charming pendant, the love of the curate for Arthur's mother, the irony is so delicate that we laugh at Arthur before we perceive that we are laughing at ourselves.

Arthur Pendennis, the son of the old apothecary and the nephew of the Major, is the character round which the various incidents of

the novel group themselves with a kind of
happy ease. He merely slips through the
world in an accidental way, but though his
adventures are without interest, the character is
drawn with such fidelity to life, and his relations
with his mother, and half sister, half love, Laura
Bell, are so natural and pleasing, that he fills
the part of hero to perfection, and if the story
is too long, it is not when we are reading about
Arthur that we think it so. His career at the
University is not distinguished ; he spends his
time with acquaintances who can afford to waste
theirs, and the result for a poor man is sufficiently serious. "The lists came out," says
Thackeray, " and a dreadful rumour ran through
the University that Pendennis of Boniface was
plucked." The element of caricature in this
Pendennis of course was not the first to see,
and he spends some time as the knight of the
rueful countenance at his mother's cottage of
Fairoaks ; but his spirits rise with the appearance on the scene of Miss Blanche Amory, the
step-daughter of Sir Francis Clavering of Clavering Hall, and he divides his attention between
paying court to her, and patronizing Laura,
whom it is his mother's wish that he should

marry. Neither of these means of passing his time having led to anything, he proceeds to London and the Temple, where he falls in with a steady companion who procures a paper for his essays, and a publisher for his novel. His uncle introduces him to polite society, and, by trading upon a family secret of the Claverings, gets him the prospect of a seat in Parliament and a rich wife. Pendennis finds out, through the treachery of his uncle's valet, to what he owes his good fortune, and refuses to advance himself by being a party to such schemes. The engagement falls through, and he returns to the woman who has waited for him, and is finally married to Laura. Such is the simple story of Arthur Pendennis ; a journalist, and not a particularly good one ; a gentleman, and not a particularly noble one ; but alive in every mood and feature, his whole body absolutely tingling with life. There has been no such portrait drawn, as Thackeray hinted, but modestly refrained from saying, since Tom Jones. Fielding's present-ment of a youth of his time is as accurate as Thackeray's of his nineteenth-century represent-ative, and about Fielding's novel there plays a breezy air of freshness which is quite foreign to

the more subtle genius of Thackeray, but the
character of Arthur Pendennis is more complicated than that of Tom Jones, and by consequence more difficult to draw. It is the
peculiarity of our high state of civilization, that
there must be many who, like Pendennis,
experience the whole range of passion and
sensation, without being able to find for them
any adequate expression. Those feelings, which
formerly only came to a man after long trouble
and thought, that complicated series of emotions
and ideas which once belonged only to philosophers and poets, have now, by the wide-spread
influence of education, become the common
property of minds that have no originality or
power. To draw such a character without
leaving the slightest opening for a charge of
inconsistency, was difficult indeed, but Thackeray never makes a mistake, and the most
trivial conversations are so literal, it is hard
to believe they did not take place. Pendennis
has been detailing to Warrington the talk of a
certain young lady, formerly an actress, whom
he met at a ball.

"'From the gravity of that woman,' he con-
cludes, 'you would have fancied she had been

born in a palace and lived all the seasons of her life in Belgrave Square.'

"'And you, I suppose you took your part in the conversation pretty well, as the descendant of the Earl your father, and the heir of Fairoaks Castle,' Warrington said. 'Yes, I remember reading of the festivities which occurred when you came of age. The Countess gave a brilliant tea soirée to the neighbouring nobility; and the tenantry were regaled in the kitchen with a leg of mutton and a quart of ale. The remains of the banquet were distributed among the poor of the village, and the entrance to the park was illuminated until old John put the candle out on retiring to rest at his usual hour.'

"'My mother is not a countess,' said Pen, 'though she has very good blood in her veins too—but commoner as she is I have never met a peeress who was more than her peer, Mr. George; and if you will come to Fairoaks Castle you shall judge for yourself of her and of my cousin too.'"

This is exactly how a high-spirited boy would have answered the badinage of his companion, and the creation of Arthur Pendennis, with his

bursts of anger, his enthusiasms, and his pride,
was an achievement in itself.

But the characters of the women in the book
do not come far behind it.   Blanche Amory,
with her *larmes* and *soupirs*, with her sensibility
and selfishness, with her elegance and her freaks
of temper, with her desire for a *grande passion*
and her deceit, almost justifies the testimonial
which her extremely candid step-father gives of
her to the Chevalier Strong.   She is an unami-
able woman, but has the interest that is common
to all the personages of fiction whom it is not
unusual to meet.   Thackeray speaks of her with
an almost unnecessary harshness, and metes out
to her at the end a justice that is more rigorous
than poetical.   He plies her, as was his habit,
with every term of endearment, and his manner
of treating " dear Blanche " is, though gentler,
not entirely dissimilar to the method he adopted
when dealing with " darling Becky."   For the
other two women he had a real and excusable
tenderness, and Laura, though slightly sketched,
has a bewitching personality.   It is a far easier
task to draw a good man than a good woman.
When we speak of a good man, we think of a
being who has the world to conquer.   A man, if

he is to be good, must possess not only great but even contradictory qualities. He must at the same time have both courage and tenderness, both reverence and strength, and if there is some difficulty in combining these excellences in one character, once that difficulty is surmounted the interest of the reader is secure. But the virtues that we love to associate with our ideal of womanhood have none of the attraction of paradox. Her true attitude in regard to matters both spiritual and of this world, is one of fond submission. She was made not to be the equal, but the helpmeet of man. She must rebel no more against her surroundings than against her fate. Tenderness is so essential a part of her that it has become proverbial ; and her courage is derived, not as man's from a consciousness of power, but from an assured belief in the right government of things, and a desire to bear unflinchingly whatever may befall. Women who possess these qualities are not colourless in life. Each of our little triumphs brings out a new wonder of admiration, and constant sorrows only serve to prove the variety of their reliant and sustaining love. But in fiction, when we try to chronicle these

similar occasions, we produce in general a sameness of effect, and Art fails to remember what
Nature has so often shown.   It required a
Shakespeare to create a Desdemona, and there
are no flawless women in the pages of Thackeray ;
Lady Castlewood is not perfect, Ethel Newcome
is fickle, and even Laura and Mrs. Pendennis
have their little fits of hardness, jealousy, and
pique.   But except for these Pendennis' mother
and betrothed are as good women as ever
passed their lives between the covers of a
book.

Many are the readers who, like Mr. Merivale,
have felt a passion for Laura, and have watched
the colour mounting to her cheeks when " Pen "
made his absurd proposal, and later her hanging
blushing on his arm, " her bright eyes beaming
with the light of love." Many are the readers
whose eyes have dimmed over the death of Mrs.
Pendennis, and who have closed the volume,
and looked back and admired the delicate shades
in this gentle picture of confiding motherhood.
The scene takes place when Warrington, in a
grand manner of his own, has just explained
that Pen was innocent in his connection with
Fanny.

I

"As for Helen, she was so delighted, that she started up, and said, 'God bless you—God for ever bless you, Mr. Warrington;' and kissed both his hands, and ran up to Pen, and fell into his arms.

"'Yes, dearest mother,' he said, as he held her to him, and with a noble tenderness and emotion, embraced and forgave her. 'I am innocent, and my dear, dear mother has done me a wrong.'

"'Oh, yes, my child, I have wronged you, thank God, I have wronged you!' Helen whispered. 'Come away, Arthur—not here— I want to ask my child to forgive me—and— and my God to forgive me; and to bless you, and love you, my son.'

"He led her, tottering, into her room, and closed the door, as the three touched spectators of the reconciliation looked on in pleased silence. Ever after, ever after, the tender accents of that voice faltering sweetly at his ear—the look of the sacred eyes beaming with an affection unutterable—the quiver of the fond lips smiling mournfully—were remembered by the young man. And at his best moments, and at his hours of trial and grief, and at his times of success and

well-doing, the mother's face looked down upon
him, and blessed him with its gaze of pity and
purity, as he saw it in that night when she yet
lingered with him. . . . .

"A little time after, it might have been a
quarter of an hour, Laura heard Arthur's voice
calling from within, 'Laura! Laura!' She
rushed into the room instantly, and found the
young man still on his knees, and holding his
mother's hand. Helen's head had sunk back
and was quite pale in the moon. Pen looked
round, scared with a ghastly terror. 'Help!
Laura, help!' he said, 'she's fainted—she's——'

"Laura screamed, and fell by the side of
Helen. The shriek brought Warrington and
Major Pendennis and the servants to the room."

The end of the year which saw the conclusion
of 'Pendennis' was occupied by Thackeray in a
curiously characteristic manner. 'Pendennis'
was a picture of society drawn with unusual
elaboration and care. It had covered a great
deal of ground; it had dealt with very large
issues; and had included in its range "a wedding
and a funeral"; but it had not omitted to look
upon these lighter things which had formed the
groundwork of 'The Book of Snobs,' and in its

method of dealing with them it had completely given the lie to his earlier manner. But for the author of 'The Kickleburys on the Rhine' 'Pendennis' might just as well not have been written. If it was necessary to produce a Christmas book, there was no necessity why this particular Christmas book should have been written. It has all the faults of 'Mrs. Perkins's Ball' and 'Our Street,' and contains an even graver indiscretion. The character of the Countess is not only an absurdity, but a feeble absurdity. Lady Rockminster in 'Pendennis' is almost too patently introduced to show that a woman may wear a coronet, and yet not be inane ; but Thackeray at least takes the trouble to draw the character, and the result is not unpleasing. Lady Knightsbridge in 'The Kickleburys' is merely a name, and we are asked to take on trust the excellences of her disposition. The introduction of this lady among the better drawn and pitiful personages of the sketch reduces the satire to a thinness beyond which it is impossible to go. The book was the subject, on its appearance, of an acute, though personal and grandiloquent review. In his 'Essay on Thunder and Small Beer' Thackeray prints the

article at length, and though he laughs at the
grandiloquence and personality, the criticisms
which he was careful to print he is careful to
leave unanswered. Indeed they were unanswer-
able, as they merely said what was patent to
every observer, that the kind of work which
might turn a penny, without credit, for an unknown writer, was unsuitable for a distinguished
novelist.

The writing of 'Esmond' formed the real
occupation of the next two years, but before
Thackeray got properly under way with it, he
found time to write a burlesque of the historical
novel. This, however, though one of the most
amazing of his numerous inconsistencies, may be
pardoned to the author of ' Rebecca and Rowena.'
It had, unlike many of ' Punch's Prize Novelists,'
the advantage of taking for its subject the work
of a writer who was no longer a contemporary,
and his admiration for Scott prevented its author
from degenerating into rudeness. It has plenty
of good humour, and is perhaps the best parody
in the language. It is interspersed with several
ballads, and that of King Canute is so excellent
as almost to reconcile us to the wanton attack on
King Richard. Athelstane, Rowena, and Sir

Wilfrid are lively and humorous comments
upon their chivalric counterparts in 'Ivanhoe,'
and Wamba jests and sings so well as to be fitted
for more serious company—

> The reddest lips that ever were kissed,
> The brightest eyes that ever have shone,
> May pray and whisper and we not list,
> Or look away and never be missed
>   Ere yet ever a month is gone.

But the man who could stop his caricature to
write verses of that quality was getting past such
frivolities.

'The History of Henry Esmond, a colonel in
the service of Her Majesty Queen Anne, written
by himself,' appeared in three volumes in the
year 1852, when Thackeray was forty-one
years of age. In several particulars it was an
effort of a quite different kind from any he had
before attempted. It followed much more nearly
than any other of his important books the
prescribed form of the novel. It was much less
a mere series of adventures ; all its incidents
contribute in their degree to shape the character,
and to influence the life of Henry Esmond ; and
the book is not, as was Thackeray's usual habit,
interspersed with detailed studies of personages

and families that have little or no bearing on the central figure of the story. It is moreover not a satire, but on the contrary a careful attempt to delineate life as it appears to the sentimental and reflective, rather than to the critical faculties of man. The form and attitude are both unfamiliar, and the success that awaited the book was not such as to induce Thackeray to return to it, until the closing years of his life, when he began 'Denis Duval.' The author of 'Esmond' gave proof of a versatility too large to be immediately understood by the public. 'Esmond' would have been a triumph for any writer ; but it was so great a triumph for the author of 'Vanity Fair' that it seemed at first almost out of the course of nature, and not to be understood. In 'Pendennis' the world had seen Thackeray at his best in the manner which he had made his own. 'Esmond' was quite unlike 'Vanity Fair' and 'Pendennis,' and the public was content to mark the difference, without admiring the versatility which was responsible ' for it.

But 'Esmond' does not only deserve praise as a humane and discerning criticism, not of society, but of life ; it is also one of the very few completely successful attempts to take the reader back into a historical period. How difficult a task this is can readily be understood when we remember the immense multitude of historical novels, and how many of them do not attempt to do anything more than to show us modern characters moving about in antique costumes, and amidst antiquated surroundings. Mr. Stevenson's 'Catriona,' however good in itself, is in this respect, as Dr. Verrall has told us,[1] completely a failure. David Balfour is a sensitive writer of the nineteenth century, condemned to masquerade as a man of action, with a rapier dangling at his side. Even in Scott the sentiments of the characters, though not essentially modern, and though seldom inconsistent, have no genuine antique flavour about them. They seem, except when he is dealing with the great characters of history, not so much to have stepped out of by-gone centuries, as to have stepped easily and naturally into them by virtue of the wide humanity of their author. But Thackeray had so steeped himself in the eighteenth century, that while we are reading 'Esmond' we seem to be listening to a sadder

[1] 'Cambridge Review,' January 25, 1894.

Addison or to a profounder Steele. The historical atmosphere is even more real than that in 'The Memoirs of Barry Lyndon,' for Redmond Barry, with all his humanity, is a monstrosity, and though he belongs to the eighteenth, would have been an unnatural product of any century.

How much of this labour, admirably spent for its purpose, was worth expending on such an object is of course another question. Shakespeare never troubled to reproduce the thoughts of the past, but was satisfied, as far as history went, if Caesar behaved as Plutarch tells us he did, or if Macbeth's actions accorded with the legend. He had no idea of making Hamlet reason as a Prince of Denmark would, or of putting into the mouth of Lear sentiments belonging properly to an early Briton. His object was not to show us Romans or Britons, Venetians or Veronese, but to put men in different situations, and to provide, by a variety of incidents, full play for the human heart. And in this he was followed by the other great Elizabethan dramatists. There are no real Romans to be found in the historical plays of Massinger or Dekker ; and few authors are ashamed when they draw Catos to let them talk the language of Whig and Tory. But whatever merit there may be in reproducing in a work of fiction the sentiments of by-gone times, that merit among others belongs to the author of 'Esmond.' Thackeray indeed seems in this book to have gone out of his way to create difficulties, and, having created them, to over-come them. It was not enough that Esmond's companions should belong to the eighteenth century, but his author, by allowing him to tell his own story, forbids himself a single opportunity of speaking in his own voice. At first sight also it appears unreasonable that a character intended to be perfect should be forced into the unpleasant position of recounting his own excellences; but even this difficulty has been partially, though only partially, overcome, and Thackeray, by the happy device of making Esmond speak at once in the first and third persons, has given the book the interest of an autobiography, without laying its hero patently open to the charge of vain-glory.

Of the book itself, of its characters, and of the fine and almost spiritual insight in it, it is impossible to speak in terms of too high a praise. To Fielding or to Scott there was

nothing difficult in life. In one the life-blood
was too warm, in the other the character was
too simple and too manly, to appreciate those
terrible alternations of emotion, which seem at
one moment to convince us of our mortality,
at the next to widen and purify the soul. Scott,
even when writing of characters long buried,
seems to live among them, and to chronicle
their careers and endings from the standpoint
of life. But in 'Esmond' Thackeray tells us
of the beauty of Beatrix, of the sympathy of
Lady Castlewood, of the roystering pleasures
of Captain Westbury and Dick Steele, as he
would speak to us of things done and "rounded
with a sleep." He does not look at death as
a state outside of life, but looks at life itself *ab
extra*, and appreciates to the full the irony, that
the Esmond who is telling us his sensations in
the little graveyard at Ealing had been dead a
hundred years. But with all this he was completely out of sympathy with those modern
ideas that would, by a kind of hopeless paradox,
reduce life to a tiresome farce, and death to its
unenviable termination. His nature was far too
sympathetic and too human not to have felt the
lachrymae rerum, but it was also far too pro-

found not to have recognized that life is a mystery, and not a puzzle, and saddest when it most nearly approaches the divine. That is why 'Esmond' is a book at once sorrowful and helpful. It is the more reverent and the more true exposition of the text he had appended to 'Vanity Fair'—*Vanitas vanitatum, omnia vanitas*.

But a work of fiction, though it may effect the purpose of a sermon or a philosophical treatise, does so by widely different means. We are not told in precise words the conclusions to be drawn from the little comedy or tragedy, but we are shown the play itself. And that we may be sufficiently interested to draw these conclusions, it is necessary that we should be deceived into imagining the actors to be real people, and the characters alive. In this Thackeray was never more successful than in his masterpiece. Most of the characters in 'Pendennis' live, it is true ; but not with the same vigour, or with, if the expression is allowable, as great a determination. Every character in 'Esmond' treats his life, whatever complexion it may wear to him, with a high and undoubting seriousness. The progress of Jesuitry is as important to Father Holt as the credit of the

victory of Wynendael to General Webb. Pleasures and wine are as real to Lord Castlewood
as her religion to his wife; and Henry Esmond
is not more deeply impressed with the solemnity
of existence than Beatrix with the pride and
delight of living. The last character is in many
respects the finest in the book, "the one incom-
parable woman," for so she has been called, "in
prose fiction"; and "surely never lighted upon
the earth a more delightful vision." There is
no more striking proof of Thackeray's knowledge of human nature than the attraction which
this character has exercised, and will continue
to exercise over his readers. She is not by
any means a good woman, yet with what an
abundant warmth she fills the solemn pages of
'Esmond.' Not since her namesake bandied
words with Benedick has any one fluttered so
gaily through her imaginary and pleasurable
youth. She was created to take captive our
delight, and, as Beatrice says, "not till God make
men of some other metal than earth" can we
fail to sympathize with Esmond's passion for
her, or to consider no pursuit too long that
might be rewarded by the possession of such a
prize.

Her brother Frank has abjured the Protestant religion, and married a foreign countess ; and this is her amazing commentary upon that occasion, with Colonel Esmond as her only auditor :—

" ' I made that onslaught on the priests,' says Miss Beatrix, afterwards, ' in order to divert my poor dear mother's anguish about Frank. Frank is as vain as a girl, cousin. Talk of us girls being vain, what are *we* to you ? It was easy to see that the first woman who chose would make a fool of him, or the first robe—I count a priest and a woman all the same. We are always caballing ; we are not answerable for the fibs we tell ; we are always cajoling and coaxing, or threatening ; and we are always making mischief, Colonel Esmond—mark my word for that, who know the world, sir, and have to make my way in it. I see as well as possible how Frank's marriage hath been managed. The Count, our papa-in-law, is always away at the coffee-house. The Countess, our mother, is always in the kitchen looking after the dinner. The Countess, our sister, is at the spinet. When my lord comes to say he is going on the campaign, the lovely Clotilda

bursts into tears, and faints—so ; he catches
her in his arms—no, sir, keep your distance,
cousin, if you please—she cries on his shoulder,
and he says, "Oh, my divine, my adored, my
beloved Clotilda, are you sorry to part with
me ? "   "Oh, my Francisco," says she, " oh my
lord ! " and at this very instant mamma and a
couple of young brothers, with moustaches and
long rapiers, come in from the kitchen, where
they have been eating bread and onions.   Mark
my word, you will have all this woman's relations at Castlewood three months after she has
arrived there.   The old count and countess, and
the young counts and all the little countesses
her sisters.   Counts! every one of these wretches
says he is a count.   Guiscard, that stabbed Mr.
Harley, said he was a count ; and I believe he
was a barber.   All Frenchmen are barbers—
Fiddlededee ! don't contradict me — or else
dancing-masters, or else priests.'   And so she
rattled on.

" 'Who was it taught *you* to dance, Cousin
Beatrix ? ' says the Colonel.

" She laughed out the air of a minuet, and
swept a low curtsey, coming up to the recover
with the prettiest little foot in the world pointed

out. Her mother came in as she was in this attitude ; my lady had been in her closet, having taken poor Frank's conversion in a very serious way; the madcap girl ran up to her mother, put her arms round her waist, kissed her, tried to make her dance, and said : 'Don't be silly, you kind little mamma, and cry about Frank turning Papist. What a figure he must be, with a white sheet and a candle, walking in a procession barefoot !' And she kicked off her little slippers (the wonderfulest little shoes with wonderful tall red heels : Esmond pounced upon one as it fell close beside him), and she put on the drollest little *moue*, and marched up and down the room holding Esmond's cane by way of taper. Serious as her mood was, Lady Castlewood could not refrain from laughing ; and as for Esmond, he looked on with that delight with which the sight of this fair creature always inspired him : never had he seen any woman so arch, so brilliant, and so beautiful.

" Having finished her march, she put out her foot for her slipper. The Colonel knelt down : 'If you will be Pope, I will turn Papist,' says he ; and her Holiness gave him gracious leave

to kiss the little stockinged foot before he put
the slipper on.

"Mamma's feet began to pat on the floor
during this operation, and Beatrix, whose bright
eyes nothing escaped, saw that little mark of
impatience.   She ran up and embraced her
mother, with her usual cry of, 'Oh, you silly
little mamma ; your feet are quite as pretty as
mine,' says she : 'they are, cousin, though she
hides 'em ; but the shoemaker will tell you that
he makes for both off the same last.'

"'You are taller than I am, dearest,' says her
mother, blushing over her whole sweet face—
'and—and it is your hand, my dear, and not
your foot he wants you to give him.'"

But with all her dainty caprice, and her charming mocks of affection, Beatrix remains worldly
and heartless.   If her character be examined
with any care, she will be found to be absolutely
incapable of an unselfish action.   Yet to become
the master of this charming shadow, this live
piece of delicate imagination, is the ambition of
every reader.   It is true, we do not love her as
she is, but we long to make her subject to an
affection, of which, when reciprocated, we feel
sure she would be worthy.   She is only heartless

K

because no man has touched her heart, only worldly because she has never felt a great emotion, only selfish because she has found it so easy to conquer,—and she might have worn her beauty humbly if she had known what was contained in the magical issues of love. Such a woman must have made a thoughtless wife to Bishop Tusher, and a bad one to Baron Bernstein ; but had Esmond asked and won her when he came back after Lille, she would have formed the true counterpart to his melancholy, and, as she borrowed strength from his manhood, would have lent new graces to his character.

With Rachel, Lady Castlewood, Esmond was too similarly‚to be excellently‚matched. That sweet lady, as she runs through the different notes of her tenderness, seems to be filled with a vague kind of passion and alarm, as if she were fluctuating between the attitudes of prizing life too highly, and valuing it not at all. The resolute Esmond, who nevertheless had won at college the name of Don Dismallo, needed another wife than this ; and his philosophical calm must often have been rudely shaken by the depths of feeling he saw revealed in Lady Castlewood. He becomes almost unmanned

when he writes of her, and his mind seems to
have caught a dye from her nature of passionate
regret.   She is always to him his "dear, dear
mistress," and her well-remembered accents inexpressibly affecting ; a pathetically human
figure, over whose memory he exhausts the
whole vocabulary of grief.   Mrs. Pendennis' love
for Arthur sustained and comforted her son.
It was so reserved and trustful, so bracing and
so healthy, that it must have contributed to
render life more simple for him, and its end
more gracious and acceptable.   But we are
alarmed by the strength of a passion that, like
Lady Castlewood's, seems to transgress the limits
of mortality.   There is no doubt, however, that
such women have existed, though no author
before Thackeray had applied himself to a
careful study of the type, and curiously enough
there is no kind of example of it to be found in
the pages of Shakespeare.   But the mind that
could watch the career of Redmond Barry, and
less than ten years later conceive and delineate
such a character as Lady Castlewood, must
have ranged through almost as great a variety
of emotions.

Henry Esmond, the hero, has been made the

subject of a good deal of comparatively undis-criminating criticism.   Thackeray himself, when irritated with the failure of his novel, consoled himself by reflecting that " after all Esmond was a prig " ; and the chance phrase has been caught up and repeated by most of his critics.   It is of course impossible to say now-a-days what mean-ing may not be attached to any word in the English language.   The employment of terms has become so loose, that it is difficult often to seize upon the precise idea which a word is intended to convey.   Mr. Trollope was of opinion that " there was that garb of melancholy over Esmond which always makes a man a prig."   But the word, as used by our old authors, is not associ-ated with any such meaning.   We find it to contain the notions of solemnity joined with pretence, a certain pomposity, perhaps, which is only half sincere.   These qualities cannot be said to exist in Henry Esmond.   He neither underrates nor over-values himself, and if he is solemn, it is his sincerity that makes him so. There was some pomposity inseparable from an attempt to chronicle one's own good behaviour, but if it was to be done, it could hardly have been done with more modesty, or with a greater

appearance of truth. Pitt Crawley was a prig,
but there is no likeness between his character
and that of Henry Esmond. It is not often, of
course, that men intended by nature for divines
wear swords at their sides, or that meditative
students of Plato win honour on the field ; but
there is nothing impossible in such a conjunction.
We do not often meet such brave and scholarly
gentlemen as Esmond ; we do not often find so
high a courage and such powers of reflection
united in one person, the capacity both to
appreciate and to despise danger ; but the in-
frequency of the occurrence should not lead us
to misunderstand it. It is only children that
object to be presented with perfect characters,
because they have not the power to differentiate
between an easily assumed appearance of virtue,
and that excellence which is only possible to one
who knows the nature of good. More mature
criticism has the power of distinguishing between
two such widely different things, and it is an
error of judgment to suppose that the man who
drew Henry Esmond and Colonel Newcome
was in danger of confounding them. Thackeray,
indeed, was never misled by hypocrisy, and in
this at least his critical faculty was always sound.

But as a critic he was not acute. He was far too inclined, having decided whether a character was good or bad, either to praise wholly, or to paint a portrait altogether black. It was not that he praised the wrong things, or blamed anything that was not blameworthy; but he forgot that as there is no one who has not deserved blame, so there is no one who has not merited praise.

In the series of lectures on the English humourists, this fault is peculiarly evident. He attacks Swift; and selects for treatment in Pope only those qualities which were really admirable. Goldsmith's good-nature, and the coarseness of Sterne, are brought out into equal relief. The result is that he tells a half-truth about these writers, and conveys what is in effect an untruth. The lectures are not in any sense critical estimates of their subjects; they are rather a series of cursory expositions of the leading impression they had produced on Thackeray's mind. They were not, however, without a good reason for being written, all the necessary material lying ready to his hand. In preparing to write 'Esmond,' he had amassed a store of information about their works and their lives, and it

was perhaps too much to expect that he should
not have been awake to so lucrative a method
of employing it. But though they contain many
sentiments that give ample proof of his sympathy
and discernment, they were quite unworthy of
the position Thackeray then occupied in the
literary world. It is hardly possible to resist
smiling when one finds Prior, Gay, and Pope
airily disposed of in forty pages, and Swift
demolished in a similar number. But the in-
adequacy of the treatment becomes ludicrous
when in a lecture gravely labelled " Hogarth,
Smollett, and Fielding," we find the author of
' Humphry Clinker' has allotted to him no
more than a page and a half. Not that it was
easy to treat, in six lectures, of twelve considerable writers, but the selection of the subject was
not imposed upon the critic. And even with
the subject selected, many of the writers chosen
need not have been dealt with. Hogarth might
well have been omitted, Gay and Prior have
little humour, while Congreve is purely a wit,
and Pope pre-eminently a poet. If these were
to be included, why not Dryden, Wycherley,
and Vanbrugh ?—and a catalogue that compre-
hended Swift might also have taken in Ben

Jonson and Shakespeare. It was not the title, however, as has been supposed, that was responsible for this discursiveness of treatment, as there are six great English humourists of the eighteenth century, and only six who without a stretch of fancy may be so called. Had Thackeray confined himself to Addison and Steele, Sterne, Fielding, Smollett, and Goldsmith, he would not only have had more space at his disposal, but he would have been saved from a serious error in classification. He might also, perhaps, have adopted an easier and more critical attitude, and would at least have been spared from finding fault with Swift because he had none of the urbanity that is peculiar to a humourist, and from reading an exaggerated kindliness into the genius of Pope. The portrait of Sterne would have remained unfair, but the critic who appreciated Fielding would have had something more to tell us of the spirit and humour of Smollett, whom he so accurately characterizes as " manly, kindly, honest, and irascible ; worn and battered, but still brave and full of heart." The lectures, as they are, are not, however, uninteresting, though they add nothing to our knowledge of the authors criticized, and

obviously cost Thackeray so little trouble, that
it is not remarkable they furnish no new index
to his mind.   They remain as a light and
pleasant interlude in his literary biography
between 'Esmond' and 'The Newcomes.'

In this latter work, noteworthy as the last of
his greater efforts, there are already to be
detected signs of a flagging pen.   He could no
longer be troubled to construct even the semblance of a story, and 'The Newcomes' is even
more rambling and discursive than 'The History
of Pendennis.'   It combines, in a curious degree,
all his previous methods.   Like 'Vanity Fair,' it
is a satire; like 'Pendennis,' it is humane; and
we meet once more the regretful weariness of
'Esmond.'   In 'Vanity Fair' we were told that
the world was a poor place to live in; in 'Pendennis' we were asked to look with pity on the
kindly race of men; while the mystery that
shadows life hangs over every page of 'Esmond.'
All these we have in 'The Newcomes,' though
its author is willing to sing, with a still higher
courage than formerly, the canticle of Nunc
Dimittis.[1]   Life is too mournfully sweet in

[1] "But above all, believe it, the sweetest Canticle is,

'Esmond' to be laid down without regret, in 'Vanity Fair' too bitter to be lived without compunction, but in 'The Newcomes' the woof is shot with so great an admixture of delight and pain, that it is no wonder Colonel Newcome says his "adsum" with a tearful acquiescence. The spirit in which the book is written is most nearly akin to that which animates 'Pendennis,' but there life is worth living, and worth leaving, because it is at once interesting and trivial. In 'The Newcomes' the same moral is drawn, because in the eyes of the author it has become both happy and sad.

Thackeray never wrote a book from an attitude more accurate or truthful. We do not always order our existence with a purpose. The least worldly of us has, like Colonel Newcome, his moments of worldliness; and the least spiritual, like Ethel, occasional glimpses of the vanity of things. We cannot be content, either always to criticize the game, or always actively to engage in it. Every one fulfils in turn the functions both of player and spectator. In

---

Nunc dimittis; when a Man hath obtained worthy Ends and Expectations."—Bacon, 'Essays': Of Death.

'The Newcomes' these truths are not made palpable merely by a contrariety of characters; the tone of the book is saturated with them, and every accent seems to tell of the reality and unreality of things. He is describing the everyday incident of the departure of a passenger ship for India :—" I scarce perceived at the ship's side beckoning an adieu, our dear old friend, when the lady whose husband had bidden me lead her away from the ship, fainted in my arms. Poor soul! Her too has fate stricken. Ah, pangs of hearts torn asunder, passionate regrets, cruel, cruel partings! Shall you not end one day ere many years; when the tears shall be wiped from all eyes, and there shall be neither sorrow nor pain ? " And so on, and so on ; mingling the earthly and the spiritual, whenever an occasion presents itself, till "Boy" says Our Father.

The novel, as Mr. Trollope has truly observed, is more a number of scattered pages from the biography of a family, than a series of related incidents. It begins by telling us all about the Newcomes, who they were and how descended, and having introduced the Colonel as an old man, takes us back to trace his childhood and his youth. Thomas Newcome, an old Indian colonel, has returned home with a pension, to spend his declining years with his son. He is anxious that the young man should follow his own inclinations, and though he has set his heart on seeing him married, is indifferent as to what profession he may choose. His son Clive falls in love with his cousin, and the father strains every endeavour to forward the match, but circumstances fall out awkwardly, and Clive makes, at Colonel Newcome's instigation, a hopeless *mésalliance*. The book closes leaving Clive a widower and an orphan, and wrapped up, as his father before him, in his boy. All this misery happens naturally enough. Had Ethel Newcome not been ambitious, or the Colonel not over-elated by his prosperity, none of it need have happened. It is not the greatest causes that in life produce the most disastrous effects.

These two personages, Colonel and Miss Newcome, have given the book its fame, but the canvas is literally crowded with every variety of men and women. Hobson Newcome is a staid and ultra-respectable man of business, while Sir Brian is a type of the sedate and prosperous London merchant. Ridley is a sensitive and delicate genius, and Frederic Baynham a jovial specimen of good-nature and *bourgeoisie*. Lord Kew is as good a portrait as could be drawn of an English aristocrat ; Clive of a youth of education and imaginative sensibility ; and the Comte de Florac of a human and pleasure-loving foreigner. The dowager Lady Kew is a woman of great age, with no thoughts but those of worldly advancement ; and Leonore, Madame de Florac, a beautiful example of patience and resignation. Rosey is a poor affectionate little thing bewildered by the tyranny of Mrs. Mackenzie ; and Mrs. Hobson Newcome a sufficiently familiar hunter of celebrities ; while Sir Barnes, the hypocritical lecturer on the affections, is well contrasted with the fiery and reckless Lord Highgate.

Among this crowd Thackeray wanders on, observing their different actions sometimes aimlessly, but never without a keen perception of their meaning. There are so many of them, that we only see parts of their careers ; and just as acquaintance after acquaintance slips out of our actual lives, and we hardly pause to ask what has become of them, so these shadowy people cross our vision for a moment, and are gone.

" They were alive," says Thackeray, " and I heard their voices, but five minutes since was touched with their grief. And have we parted with them here on a sudden, and without so much as a shake of the hand ? "   Ethel Newcome, he condescends to hint to us, was ultimately united to Clive, and it is with a thrill of pleased recognition that we find them masquerading together in the background of ' Philip.' But for the most of them, he leaves the skein where he dropped it, and we may spin or tangle it as we will.

Clive Newcome, the nominal hero, round whose career and marriage the main incidents of the novel are grouped, forms an interesting addition to Thackeray's commentary on the youth of the nineteenth century.   It is difficult not to be reminded of Arthur Pendennis.   Both are the descendants of gentle families, moving in a higher society than that of their origin ; both are indolent, though they have fits of intermittent industry ; both are fully alive to the influences of literature and art.   One has lost a mother, one a father ; and Mrs. Pendennis' devotion to Arthur is as intense as that of Colonel Newcome for Clive.   Both natures find the restraint of a

regular profession intolerably irksome. They
have many of the same virtues; both are
gentlemen, and they both comport themselves
well in trying situations.

But the difference between them is more
striking than the similarity. Arthur Pendennis
considers Mrs. Pendennis' devotion to him to
be little more than his due; Clive is always
profoundly grateful for his father's love.
Arthur is capable of serious indiscretions; he
proposes to make an absurd marriage with
Miss Costigan, and his treatment of Fanny is
so thoughtless as to be almost cruel. The less
robust Clive never deviates from the paths of
strict propriety. Arthur takes years to find
out that the one woman suited to be his mate
has been long waiting at his door, and he
finally obtains her when it appeared that he
had become entangled with Blanche Amory.
Clive never swerves from his devotion to Ethel,
whom he cannot obtain, and he marries another
not from caprice, but out of deference to his
father's wishes. Arthur is self-confident, and in
no danger of underrating his powers; Clive
is diffident almost to a fault. Arthur attains
success; Clive, failure. Clive shrinks at the

first touch of misfortune ; Arthur marches
buoyantly on, confident that his ability will
ultimately be recognized. Clive is subject to
fits of melancholy, and we leave him heart-
broken by "unmerited disaster"; Arthur never
becomes more than petulant with evil fate,
and he enjoys to the full all that the present
can give. None can doubt which is the more
loveable, or which has the finer character.

Alas ! poor Clive. For a man who hopes to
succeed he commits the one fault unpardonable
by those who are busied with idle things. He
treats his life as a matter of grave importance,
and looks out soberly and sadly on the myriad
existences about him. Pendennis, more happily
dowered, turns his fancy to good account as a
journalist; Clive falls a victim to his own
imagination. He, a mere mortal, laid hands
on the fire of the Gods, and found too late
that it consumed him from within. It is
enough to contrast the fates of Clive Newcome
and Arthur Pendennis to understand what
Thackeray thought of the way of the world,
and of the cruel satire of circumstances, which
ordain that one who has ideas above his station
or capacity will inevitably fall below it.

In the actual story of the Newcomes,
however, Thackeray feared to accumulate the
tragedy, and after the death of the Colonel
he effected in a few pages the deliverance of
Clive; and we are told fairly plainly that a
dea ex machinâ descended in the person of
Ethel Newcome. This, which was no violent
outrage on probability, affords the desired
relief, though it does not render some parts of
the former conduct of Ethel any the more
comprehensible. She herself is not so dazzling
a creation as Beatrix, though far more gentle
and winning, and it is difficult to know whether
we ought to admire the art which has constructed for her her similar inconsistencies, or
wonder whether such repetitions are to be
found in Nature. Partly as a result of her
training, and partly from the influence exercised over her by the dowager Lady Kew, she
is possessed with the idea of making a brilliant
marriage. But her intentions are complicated
by the affection with which Clive Newcome
inspires her. She becomes engaged to Lord
Kew, but no sooner has she attained it, than
she is almost angry with her triumph. She
adopts towards her *fiancé* an attitude of

L

petulant suspicion, which soon ends in the rupture of the engagement. She is immediately subjected to the reproaches of Lady Kew, and being herself somewhat piqued at having lost a coronet, consents to encourage a particularly foolish young nobleman called the Marquis of Farintosh. With him also she finally breaks, having her eyes opened to the danger of such alliances by the fate of her sister-in-law, Lady Clara Pulleyn or Newcome. As it was not possible for Thackeray to repeat a third time the same situation, we are not surprised to find that Clive has meanwhile been married to Miss Mackenzie.

This is the main outline of her story ; but she fluctuates back and forward from ambition to love, and from love to ambition. If she is fifty times in one mood, she is fifty times in the other. She does not know her own wishes, and in vain tries to rationalize her desires. If Clive had not married Miss Mackenzie, it is doubtful whether she still would not have preferred to him a more aristocratic lover. That there are many girls who would act in this way is not to be denied ; and it gave an added piquancy to her case that Ethel

Newcome should be so simple and so loveable. But the character, when thus made interesting, becomes untrue. It is not easy to suppose that a girl so womanly could continue for long to act in the manner described. The scene in which she is introduced to the Colonel predisposes us in her favour. It is admirably calculated to awaken interest, without cloying it by any detailed description of her charms. "I doubt whether even the designer," says Thackeray, "can make such a portrait of Miss Ethel Newcome as shall satisfy her friends and her own sense of justice. That blush which we have indicated, he cannot render. How are you to copy it with a steel point and a ball of printer's ink? That kindness which lights up the Colonel's eyes; gives an expression to the very wrinkles round about them; shines as a halo round his face,—what artist can paint it? The painters of old, when they portrayed sainted personages, were fain to have recourse to compasses and gold-leaf—as if celestial splendour could be represented by Dutch metal! As our artist cannot come up to this task, the reader will be pleased to let his fancy paint for itself the look of courtesy for a woman, admiration for a young beauty, protection for an innocent child, all of which are expressed upon the Colonel's kind face, as his eyes are set upon Ethel Newcome.

"'Mamma has sent us to bid you welcome to England, uncle,' says Miss Ethel, advancing, and never thinking for a moment of laying aside that fine blush which she brought into the room, and which is *her* pretty symbol of youth, and modesty, and beauty.

" He took a little slim white hand and laid it down on his brown palm, where it looked all the whiter ; he cleared the grizzled mustachio from his mouth, and stooping down he kissed the little white hand with a great deal of grace and dignity. There was no point of resemblance, and yet a something in the girl's look, voice, and movements, which caused his heart to thrill, and an image out of the past to rise up and salute him. The eyes which had brightened his youth (and which he saw in his dreams and thoughts for faithful years afterwards, as though they looked at him out of heaven) seemed to shine upon him after five-and-thirty years. He remembered such a fair bending neck and clustering hair, such a light foot and airy figure, such a slim hand lying in his own——and now parted from it with a gap of ten thousand long days between."

This is a modest maid, who might well in after life have been dazzled by ambition, and for whom the committal of one serious flirtation was quite a possibility ; but she could hardly, as Thackeray would have us believe, have remained in reality the same, and been subject to recurrent attacks of a craving for an alliance only capable of conferring social distinction. " For her," he says in another place, " the world began at night ; when she went in the train of the old Countess from hotel to hotel, and danced waltz after waltz with Prussian and Neapolitan secretaries, with princes' officers of ordonnance— with personages even more lofty very likely—for the Court of the Citizen King was then in its splendour ; and there must surely have been a number of nimble young royal highnesses who would like to dance with such a beauty as Miss Newcome. The Marquis of Farintosh had a share in these polite amusements. His English conversation was not brilliant as yet, although his French was eccentric ; but at the court balls, whether he appeared in his uniform of the

Scotch Archers, or in his native Glenlivat tartan, there certainly was not in his own or the public estimation a handsomer young nobleman in Paris that season. It has been said that he was greatly improved in dancing ; and, for a young man of his age, his whiskers were really extraordinarily large and curly.

" Miss Newcome, out of consideration for her grandmother's strange antipathy to him, did not inform Lady Kew that a young gentleman by the name of Clive occasionally came to visit the ' Hôtel de Florac.'"

The critic can hardly fail to observe that much of Ethel Newcome's attraction consists in the combination of qualities which are not usually found together.

With Colonel Newcome it is different, though we should be far less likely to meet with anything approaching him in actual life. But it is the strength of his qualities that is rare, not their existence in one person. Generosity, magnanimity, and gusts of noble rage belong often to the same man. Though a magnanimity as great as Colonel Newcome's is seldom seen, if we did see it anywhere, we should almost expect to find along with it the other constituents of his character. Colonel Newcome is like the giants in the children's books ; they are exactly like human beings, only larger. They have all the features, and even wear the clothes of humanity, and we are aware of a certain loss in innocence and faith, when we cease to believe in these reasonable monsters. So well in Colonel Newcome is the resemblance preserved, that we feel that even in his best moments we are capable of imitating him. He acts just as we should like to act, and very much as we should act, if we were always able to obey the higher instincts of our nature. He does not pretend to be perfect ; he has little of the reserve and self-control of Esmond ; and he gives way more than once to passionate anger and grief. But his motives never fail to be generous, and the same want of calculation that weakens his judgment gives freer play to his heart. Henry Esmond, with a few alterations, might have lived two thousand years ago, and we catch traces in him of the stoic acquiescence, and the pagan feeling for beauty, which belonged to Marius the Epicurean. But Colonel Newcome could hardly have flourished before the beginning of our century. In

some respects he recalls the knights of the
middle ages, but he has lost much of their
enthusiasm and certainty. He does not take
himself sufficiently seriously to belong to an
early civilization, and though as simple and
trustful as a child, has no idea of his individuality playing any considerable part in the
ordered scheme of things. He is a true product
of a later Christianity, as clear of fanaticism as
he is innocent of doubt. He is not troubled
with much philosophy, but he has enough to
suffer bravely and to live like an honest man,
and the scene at his death-bed is deservedly one
of the most famous in fiction. It is not only
that it is told with a kind of haunting pathos,
and a tender felicity of phrase, but its dignified
tragedy gives consistency and completeness to
the rambling incidents of the book. And just
as we are unable to judge of a career till it is
finished, it is only when we close 'The Newcomes' that we clearly appreciate the accuracy
of its criticism of life. We are reminded of the
words of Mr. Stevenson :—" The sights and
thoughts of my youth pursue me ; and I see
like a vision the youth of my father, and of his
father, and the whole stream of lives flowing

down with the sound of laughter and tears. And I admire and bow my head before the romance of destiny."

With 'The Newcomes' off his hands, Thackeray gave up the next two years to writing occasional verses and papers, and lecturing in different cities. None of these occupations was new. Whenever he had leisure, he was a frequent contributor to the magazines, and he continually interspersed his tales with verses and ballads. His claims to rank as a poet have often been considered, and settled with a remarkable unanimity. It is allowed on all sides that the volume of his collected verses contains nothing of high poetic quality, and is distinguished by none of those powers of contemplation and directness which belong to the highest poetry. But it is also admitted that his verses, though never magical, are often charming, and always bear the stamp of their author. The tone, in general, is one of smiling melancholy, as if the laughing and weeping philosophers were to perform their functions at once. His poems would not by themselves have secured for Thackeray a high place in literature, but some of them are not likely to be readily for-

gotten.   As a poet, his range was neither wide
nor particularly deep, but his touch is gentle
and true.   His attitude is characteristically
shown in the 'Ballad of Bouillabaise,' or in

> " The story of two hundred years
>   Writ on the parchment of a drum,"

but it is perhaps seen best in ' The Pen and the
Album.' The pen is supposed to be speaking :—

> " I've helped him to pen many a line for bread,
>   To joke with sorrow aching in his head,
>   And make your laughter when his own heart bled.

> " I've spoke with men of all degree and sort,
>   Peers of the land, and ladies of the Court.
>   Oh, but I've chronicled a deal of sport,

> " Feasts that were ate a thousand days ago,
>   Biddings to wine that long hath ceased to flow,
>   Gay meetings with good fellows long laid low.

> " Summons to bridal, banquet, burial, ball,
>   Tradesman's polite reminder of his small
>   Account due Christmas last—I've answered all."

The note is that of Omar Khayyam.   But he
is not given over to sadness, and occasionally
he seems to remember that he ought to be comforted.   Then a merrier mood supervenes, and
he can afford to break his jest about the inevit-

able Christmas bill. Occasionally he begins a
verse in the highest of spirits, but his voice is
apt to break.

> " He, by custom patriarchal,
>   Loved to see the beaker sparkle,
>   And he thought the wine improved
>   Tasted by the lips he loved,
>   By the kindly lips he loved."

The added tenderness of the last line fore-
shadows the bitterness of regret.

Of his prose works, there is none of any importance between ' The Rose and the Ring,'
published in 1855, and ' The Virginians,' which
did not appear till 1858. ' The Rose and the
Ring ' is a fairy story for children, but it does
not contain much that was peculiar to Thackeray, and ends, as by nature bound, with the
general happiness of every one. But of its kind,
as Mr. Lang prettily observes, " it is indispens-
able in every child's library, and parents should
be urged to purchase it at the first opportunity,
as without it no education is complete."[1] It is
also interesting as throwing additional light on
Thackeray's character, and was the outcome of
the same feelings that find expression in the

[1] ' The Yellow Fairy Book ' : Preface.

concluding paragraph of 'The Newcomes.' "The poet of Fableland," he says there, "rewards and punishes absolutely. He splendidly deals out bags of sovereigns, which won't buy anything; belabours wicked backs with awful blows, which do not hurt; endows heroines with preternatural beauty, and creates heroes who, if ugly sometimes, yet possess a thousand good qualities, and usually end by being immensely rich; makes the hero and heroine happy at last, and happy ever after. Ah, happy, harmless Fableland, where these things are! Friendly reader! may you and the author meet there on some future day! He hopes so; as he yet keeps a lingering hold of your hand, and bids you farewell with a kind heart." Here is an author who does not fly to fairy tales for relief from the harshness of the world, but who sees in them, with a fine intuition, a justification for its existence.

'The Virginians,' the sequel to 'Esmond,' is one of the longest of Thackeray's books, and the only one which it is almost impossible to read as a whole. The story of 'The Newcomes' was not constructed with care, but compared with that of 'The Virginians' it is a model of what a plot should be. But it was necessary,. if the public was to be amused, to write something new ; and as Thackeray's invention had begun to fail him, there was nothing for it but to revivify, as best he could, the dry bones of a former tale. For this, as there was no one in ' Vanity Fair' whose fortunes were sufficiently interesting, and as Mr. and Mrs. Arthur Pendennis had begun to weary us in ' The Newcomes,' there was nothing left but to return to the house of Castlewood, and to find there his opportunity. In ' Esmond' he had lingered round its old grey walls till every stone of them had become familiar, and he must have caught at the idea, when it occurred to him, of peopling them again with a younger generation. The novel, indeed, begins with vivacity enough. Henry Warrington rings the same bell his grandfather had so often rung ; the fountain in the courtyard plashes again ; and the momentary appearance of Madame Bernstein adds reality to the illusion. But as the novel proceeds, it loses its connection. We are spirited across from England to America, and from America to England ; people whom we had looked upon as dead come suddenly to life ;.

and of the brothers it is not clear which interests us most at odd moments, or least in the end. And though it was not inartistic that we should catch a glimpse of Beatrix in her old age, the Baroness Bernstein is far too much in evidence. She is the central figure of 'The Virginians.' Again and again we are invited to mark the results of selfishness and caprice, and the old sinner with her rouge and her cards points a moral too obvious and dull. The chief effect of the character is to destroy much of the illusion of 'Esmond,' but uncalled-for as it is, it is drawn with more care than any other in the book. Henry and George, the Castlewood family, are not colourless, it is true ; but they have little consistency or vigour about them, while Theo and Hetty are vague almost to faintness.

With the historical personages, Thackeray is in general more successful, and there are many charming glimpses of the eighteenth-century fribbles and wits. But the attempt to portray the youth of George Washington is not even seriously made. 'The Virginians' is a book to dip into and to glance at occasionally with profit, but it is too lengthy and too purposeless to claim attention as a whole. It serves as a good example to show how useless are great faculties of wisdom and discernment, when unallied with a sense of order and proportion. The truth is, all good novels present to us the world in miniature, and the figures, unless we get some hint of a scheme behind them, interest us no more than shadows on a wall. A tale "full of sound and fury, signifying nothing," is precluded by its nature from giving an accurate representation of life. It was not that Thackeray did not know this, but his pen and brain were weary, and he was becoming incapable of taking a wide view of the large subjects with which he still endeavoured to grapple.

In 'The Four Georges,' a series of lectures delivered some time before, but not published till 1860, this fault is beginning to be evident, all the more, perhaps, because it was a topic on which he was constitutionally incapable of being heard to advantage. Had he written the lectures at the time when his interest in life was at its keenest and freshest, he could hardly have done justice to the four Georges. He never saw anything in a king, except a very ordinary

mortal, dressed out with pomposity and conceit ;
but in ' The Four Georges ' he makes no attempt
to cope with the difficulties of his task. It was
natural that he should not view them as rulers,
but he might at least have attempted to present
to us a connected idea of their careers. He
who would turn the pages of ' The Four
Georges ' to learn anything of parliamentary
government would only lose his labour for his
pains ; but the reader who expected to find
there what manner of men they were, who were
so greatly responsible for modern England,
would commit an equally grave, though more
natural mistake. Unlike ' The ,Virginians,' the
lectures are interesting reading, but, like ' The
Virginians,' they suffer from their author's never
having had a clear idea of what he was
engaged in describing. They consist rather in
gossip about the habits of the four Georges
than in criticism of their policy, or in portraits
of the men.

Of the other two books of this period, reminiscent also of his earlier work, there is little to
be said. One, ' Lovel the Widower,' was no
more than a rehabilitation of a dramatic fragment called ' The Wolves and the Lamb,' written

in 1854. The plot is almost identical, and in the original it was so farcical and harsh, that it was next door to impossible to make anything of it. But what patience could effect has been done, and 'Lovel the Widower' is the best of the stories that properly belong to the period of 'Mrs. Perkins's Ball' and 'The Kickleburys on the Rhine.' But even then it was a poor kind of achievement for the author of 'Pendennis' and 'The Newcomes.' Mrs. Prior, a pilferer of sugar, and her daughter, a reformed and hypocritical ballet-girl, are not pleasant people to contemplate, and many of the other characters, like Lady Baker, are sordid in their self-importance and vulgarity. The kindliness of his later manner, and the interest of his digressions, were powerless to construct from these a kindly or interesting story.

With his other tale, 'The Adventures of Philip,' they were more successful; and, in its way, to transform Caroline Gann into the little sister said much for his creative genius. But the novel, which might have been good, is marred all through by having to carry along with it several of the melodramatic characters from the unfortunate 'Shabby Genteel Story.'

M

George Brandon was not likely to have turned
out better than Dr. Firmin, and the parson who
celebrated the mock marriage might have ended
his career as Mr. Tufton Hunt ; but when we
consider 'Philip' by itself, these characters are
not to be admired. If George Brandon could
have existed so could Firmin, but the one is as
extravagant as the other, and the surroundings
which were natural to both were not worth
depicting. Even the good people catch a taint
from the atmosphere in which these worthies
move, and Arthur Pendennis and Laura have
so little of their old charm that we wonder why
they should have been dragged from their quiet
and cosy corner.

But the book is not without a biographical
interest, inasmuch as it is merely a *réchauffée* of
many earlier productions. Philip Firmin's adventures are not altogether unlike those of Pendennis, but he is a loud and noisy person, whose
literary efforts must have been astonishingly
bald. The Earl of Ringwood is a more violent
edition of the Marquis of Steyne, and the
publisher in the book is, what one would hardly
have thought possible, a caricature of Bungay
and Bacon. Charlotte is a mixture of Theo

Lambert and Amelia Sedley, and for Philip's misadventure at the ball we have to go as far back as 'The Memoirs of George Fitzboodle.' In hardly any instance is the repetition an improvement, and the book, which added nothing to Thackeray's reputation, contains hardly anything that was new. It was the last of his imaginative works which he was destined to complete.

There remain besides, as the fruit of his declining years, only the unfinished fragment of 'Denis Duval,' and 'The Roundabout Papers,' which with their fine spirit of humanity and calm, form a fitting close to his life.

" A big, fierce, weeping, hungry man," says Carlyle, summing up his view of Thackeray, " not a strong one ; " and the judgment, if inaccurate, is sufficiently luminous to help us to understand him. It has the merit, among others, of suggesting that we should fix our attention rather on the writer than on his writings, for it is Thackeray, and not the work for which he was responsible, that has left so large a mark upon our time. His personality is always to the front, and it is not life so much as

his view of it which we see in his novels. At
bottom he was more a preacher than an artist; and
if we were only to look at his books separately,
and to judge of them as works of art, we should
form a wrong estimate of his probable influence.
In any serious attempt to ascertain his place in
literature, we should have to consider not only
his novels, but the whole character of their
author as it appears to us in them. But this,
as far as the works are concerned, is what has
been attempted in the foregoing pages, and
before proceeding to lay down anything about
his character as a whole, and free from the en-
cumbrance of being only able to touch on it in-
cidentally, while dealing with his tales and novels
in chronological succession, it will be convenient
to summarize what has been said.

Till the publication of 'Barry Lyndon' he
wrote nothing which, by itself, has interest for
posterity. The Yellowplush papers and corre-
spondence, 'Cox's Diary,' 'The Fatal Boots,' and
the whole series of satires and novelettes which
he produced at that period, were purely ephemeral.
A parody so long as 'Catherine,' a tale so sordid
as the 'Shabby Genteel Story,' a novelette so
ineffective as 'The Great Hoggarty Diamond,'

would by themselves have given no author lasting reputation. And even 'Barry Lyndon,' it must be repeated, though a remarkable production, has few of the qualities of a work of the first excellence. It will be read, perhaps, as long as ' Jonathan Wild,' but it is not to ' Jonathan Wild ' that Fielding owes his fame. ' The Book of Snobs,' and the novelettes dealing with that genus, chiefly appealed to the generation for which they were written, and they will soon cease to have any but a historical interest. Nor are ' The Virginians ' and ' Philip ' likely to fare any better, and nobody who was merely looking for a good novel would trouble himself with them.

But when we come to ' Vanity Fair,' to ' Pendennis,' and ' The Newcomes,' we raise a more serious question. Here we have books which, at the first sight, might appear to be sufficiently good to stand alone. A great many qualities, however, are necessary for literary immortality, and in some these three novels are notoriously deficient. In the first place, they extend without exception to far too great a length, and though they might hold the reader's interest from monthly number to monthly number, when

published as a whole they are only readable
with difficulty.   In the second, 'Pendennis' and
'The Newcomes' are constructed with so little
art, that we should not be surprised if the conclusion arrived with any chapter, or was never
reached at all ; and even in 'Vanity Fair,' the
fall of Becky, the natural termination of the
book, occurs about the middle of the second
volume.   They seem, both in plot and in method,
to be the work of chance, whereas in every
really great work of art "the ideal in all its
completeness governs the whole process ; and
there is not, from the very outset, one arbitrary
stroke, one note or touch, that is not instinct
with the power of the whole, and prophetic of
its fulfilment." [1]   The result is, that even with all
their merits these defects alone would make us
hesitate to predict that any one of them would
for its own sake continue to be read, whereas
we would turn to 'The Scarlet Letter' and 'Old
Mortality,' if Scott and Hawthorne had written
nothing else.   This happy fate, the power of for
ever compelling readers by its own intrinsic
excellence, belongs to only one of Thackeray's
books, 'The History of Henry Esmond.'

[1] Principal Caird : 'The Philosophy of Religion.'

But even without it, his great works would never have wanted for an audience, and it would be safe to say that he will remain a classic, not on account of any of them, but because of all. The author of 'Pendennis' can be studied in 'The Newcomes,' and in 'Pendennis' the author of 'Vanity Fair,' and, even in his minor productions, the character of Thackeray. None of these works would have made its author a classic, but they are each classical because they were written by him. With all his faults, there has been no such genius engaged in novel-writing since the death of Scott, none with such width of discernment, and so humane an understanding of life. He has left a very different body of work, it is true; but it will all repay study, as the production of an author who had much that is vital to say, not only to his own generation, but to those that come after. Hard as the task, from an artistic standpoint, may appear, it will be readily undertaken by multitudes as long as our civilization remains approximately the same. A writer who so constantly "knocks directly at the door of our tears," who has so great a command over our modern emotions, may express himself in any form he

pleases, and yet not forfeit his claim to our
attention. In his excellences and defects he
remains the prose epitome of our century.

The complexity of his character has already
been adverted to ; and his infelicities were
almost as great as his successes. 'Esmond'
was beyond the reach of Scott, but 'Catherine'
was equally far below it. Lady Castlewood is
as spiritual as any of Hawthorne's creations,
but Becky Sharp might have been painted by
Hogarth ; and 'The Book of Snobs' is occupied
entirely with the exterior of things.

If one might borrow terms from philosophy,
Thackeray was a dualist. For him there were
two worlds ; he was not "pure air and fire," and
the "dull elements of earth and water" were
also constituents of his being. When we read
Fielding, we think of nothing but the body, its
clothes and its affections. Man in his pages is
the highest of the animals, but still an animal.
When we read Shakespeare or Hawthorne, we
form no accurate idea what the different people
are like, we seem to know them themselves, to
be familiar, not with their persons, but with
their thoughts. So much is this so, that we are
not offended to see Hamlet played on two

consecutive nights by different actors, and no one ever wasted a moment on computing the income of Miriam or Zenobia. But for Thackeray, the exterior of the character had as much attraction as the character itself. His greatest tragedy, that of 'The Newcomes,' is brought about by the loss of money ; and Henry Esmond, who remains for us the pure idea of a melancholy commentator on life, has his face marred by the ravages of small-pox.

A similar attitude is noticeable in his treatment of greater things. At one moment he seems to be full of the joy of existence, at the next to be reminding us that we must not value it too highly ; and his transitions from the material to the spiritual are almost startlingly abrupt. He loved the world, yet he was always preaching its vanity, and though he constantly adjures us to look beyond, he accentuates, rather than conceals, the bitterness of parting with it. It is for this reason that he is so modern, and, like Tennyson, represents both our weakness and our strength. He does not speak to us from the calm heights of Wordsworth, and he has none of Mr. Arnold's cold decision, for his character was not purely contemplative, and he was far more akin to the Hebrews than the Greeks. But his voice, though it may be broken with tears, is never without its note of hope and consolation.

" Oh the sad old pages," he writes in one of his last papers, "the dull old pages. Oh the cares, the ennui, the squabbles, the repetitions, the old conversations over and over again ! But now and again a kind thought is recalled, and now and again a dear memory. Yet a few chapters more, and then the last, after which behold Finis itself come to an end, and the Infinite begun."

Who is there who does not recognize in the writer of that passage a humanity and a reverence that are found in conjunction only in the greatest minds ?

CHAPTER IV

STYLE AND GENERAL CHARACTERISTICS

THAT it should be considered necessary to write anything on the style of an author, on the turn of his periods, or on the arrangement of his sentences, is one of the curiosities of literary criticism. But we live at a time in which some such criticism is particularly demanded.

At first sight it appears almost too clear for demonstration, that the style and the author are one and the same, and that as in the art of speaking in public, if a man has nothing to say he will never learn to say it. But the truth of this axiom has been constantly disputed, and there have been periods in all countries, in which it has been thought that all that was necessary for excellence as a writer, was a power of tormenting the language with sufficient grace. But the quality of greatness is in itself peculiar, and it follows that great orators and writers, when they express their ideas naturally, use a form and manner not common to common men. Their habits of thinking are the cause of their style, and it is a fallacy that would be obvious if less frequent to suppose that we shall arrive at a similar result by any study of the effect.

The fallacy, nevertheless, has obtained credit with many considerable writers. Ever since the time of Euphues, there have been found, at recurrent intervals, various schools of authors, professing the same objects as those who are now content to be known, as if in ridicule of their claims, by the barbarous appellation of " stylists." The study of style by itself labours under two grave disadvantages. In the first place the object of the study, which is a living imitation, is unattainable, and in the second it is bound to produce a nerveless and affected literature. It would almost seem that the students of this art supposed that language was not the natural vehicle of thought, and that it was as difficult for a man to learn to write, as for an infant to learn to speak. The truth is of course quite the other way, and reading does not more easily

make a full man, than a full man expresses his
thoughts. If a man has anything to say, to say
it is only difficult if he has confused his mind
and cramped his fingers, by studying how it
may best be done.

Towards the end of the eighteenth century,
when there was a singular and healthy absence
of writing about writing itself, there was hardly
an author who was not the possessor of a blame-
less and perspicuous style. Let any one open
at hazard any of the introductions to the poetical
translations so common then, or any volume on
travel or government, and he will find that
however inconsiderable the writer, whatever he
has got to say he has no difficulty in saying
with simplicity and force. Even Johnson, a
considerable offender against simplicity, was well
aware of its value, and selected the pages of
Addison as the model of English prose. It has
been commonly said that Johnson thought in
Saxon, and wrote in Latin, phraseology. But
this is far from a complete explanation, and the
elephantine tread of his earlier style is only an
exaggeration of the cumbrousness of his ideas,
and arose in great part from the necessity of
saying something new on social subjects that

had been fully dealt with before. In the 'Lives of the Poets,' where he broke ground comparatively fresh, and on which he had thought much and often, his style more resembles pointed conversation than his previous contributions to the ' Rambler.' To take another instance ; Milton, it has been said with obvious truth, is a great master of style, and there are many passages in Milton not free from the charge of straining after effect ; but in the main he writes as he thinks, and where the construction of the lines is remarkable, the thoughts that inform them are generally unique.

And this will be found to mark the difference between the style of a great author, and the laboured language of a " stylist." In every book passages must occur where the reader's attention is arrested, and these will be found on re-perusal to contain, either a striking thought, or a series of sentences artificially arranged. The one, if words be used in their proper sense, is style, the other, artifice. Thackeray, as much as any author since Addison or Swift, is a master of style, free, simple, and easy, narrating the simplest things in the simplest manner, rising to such heights of grandeur as his mind

was susceptible of, and moving responsive to
every mood of his capacious tenderness. Always
his servant, never his master, what he thought it
said with so literal an exactness as to make him
in one sense the most truthful of writers.   If he
descends into caricature, he alone is responsible ;
if his power of discrimination is lost in abuse it
is not his style that has hurried him away.   Of
such a style, so unobtrusive, so obedient, if a
critic were anxious to be paradoxical, he would
say it did not exist.   But that Thackeray has
no style is only true in the sense in which it is
the highest compliment that can be paid him.
He has no mannerisms which he has made his
own, no phrases of which he cannot rid himself,
no tricks of arranging his particles or postponing
the introduction of his verbs.   Even when he
indulges in the repetition of a word, and makes
Barry Lyndon speak of his "poor dear, dear
little boy," or Esmond of his "dear, dear mistress," the charm consists in the absence of any
studied artifice, in the expression being there by
an accidental overflow of affection.   Neither is
his habit of familiarly addressing the reader a
trick of style, it is a mannerism exceedingly
characteristic, and more a fault of thought than

of language. Its frequent occurrence, however
irksome, is never unnatural. The pen talks to
the reader, because the author is determined to
treat him as a companion.

It is true, no doubt, that the critical reader
would recognize any long quotation from
Thackeray as the work of his hand, and so
far he has a manner of his own, but every good
author has as much as this.   The prose of
Bacon, and even of Addison, is recognizable,
and even where a writer's range is far wider
than Thackeray's, there is still in every considerable passage the imprint of his hand.
There is a literature about the doubtful plays of
Shakespeare founded on internal evidence alone.
Other authors who have become the devotees
of their style could be recognized even if the
sense of the passage were altered.   There are
many passages of Mr. Stevenson's that we
would know to be borrowed in whatever context
they were found.   "At the best of it," says
Mr. Stevenson, "there was an icy place about my
heart, and life seemed a black business to be
at all engaged in.   For two souls in particular
my pity flowed."   And again : " Of a sudden her
face appeared in my memory, the way I had

first seen it, with the parted lips; at that, weakness came in my bosom and strength into my legs." This is a kind of effective writing in which Thackeray never indulges. Where he has a plain statement to make, he makes it plainly, and his unembellished narrative depends on reflection and incident alone. By this means occasionally he is dull, but he never wearies. The attention of his readers may sometimes stray, but their interest is never palled, and he is saved entirely from that tendency which in varying degrees is so fatal to modern prose— to sacrifice even sense and dignity upon the "altar of art."

Of the other portion of this chapter, of the general characteristics of Thackeray, it is not so easy to speak. The subject "bristles with commonplace," which though not absolutely correct, and consequently not safely to be ignored, is based, in the main, on a fair estimate of the author. All therefore that here can be done is to go over ground, of necessity familiar, and to deal with topics on which the current notions contain an unusual degree of truth.

The early part of Thackeray's life, after he

N

had settled down to a literary career, was spent amid Bohemian surroundings. A solitary man, left alone with his children, he sought relaxation amid a bachelor society. His university career was short, and never having been a member of a regular profession, his acquaintanceships until a later period were mostly formed among those of similar tastes and occupations. Part of his life he spent in clubs, part in that large district called Bohemia, and part as a solitary student. The environment of a romance writer is of little consequence, because his business has no connection with affairs, but for a novelist it is of the first importance. The author of a novel of manners which professedly depicts society, can hardly be said to be equipped for his task unless he has seen "all sorts and conditions of men," and travels as wide as those of Ulysses would form no useless part of his education. It is the duty of a novelist to see life, and to see it whole. A partial study of a restricted area has its use no doubt, but it is apt to lead to mistakes that the mere student would not be tempted to commit. A man by nature reflective, meditating on the abyss of Bohemianism which he saw around him, might

well think Dr. Brand Firmin and his *confrères*
possible and even likely characters ; to the man
of the world, as to the philosopher, they seem
so improbably detestable as not to be worth
depicting.

Thackeray's early life indeed furnished a poor
training for the work by which he has become a
classic, and it explains much that is wanting in
his novels, and much that ought not to have
been there.   What he saw of Bohemia afforded
material for some of his least agreeable sketches,
and the influence of his sojourn in club-land is
plainly discernible in ' The Book of Snobs,' and
even, though there much more happily, in ' Pendennis.'   The strange rivalry between Lady
Castlewood and Beatrix as objects of Esmond's
affection, though worked out with such charms
as hardly to displease, is a product of the study.
Theoretically there is nothing impossible in the
situation, and the reader is content to believe
that a man might be in love with both mother
and daughter at the same time, but that Esmond
should pay his addresses to the one, and ultimately marry the other, offends those who are
unable to remember such an instance of raptur-
ous and methodical affection.

Some such connection there must be between the circumstances of a novelist and the scenes he makes familiar by the exercise of his art, but in Thackeray's case the connection is unusually close.   He depicted what he saw, and where his experience failed him he fell back upon his imagination, only to return to his experience when his imagination was exhausted.   He had no notion of supplementing the one by the other, to fill up a preconcerted list of scenes and characters, that it is highly improbable he ever made.   If it was possible to do without a plan, he did without it, and if he did not happen to need a character to complete a scene, he rarely troubled his invention.   He had seen some doubtful journalists, and there are doubtful journalists in plenty in his books, but he introduces us to no author who is both a scholar and a gentleman. In ' The Newcomes ' we fall upon a large company of artists ; they are all, however, of the class with whom he might have come in contact in his youth.   Yet he must have known that there were living many celebrated painters who were socially quite his equals ; nor is there any reason easily discoverable why Ridley, the only artist of ability mentioned in the novel, should have

been the offspring of a cook. In his novels of
society none of his characters seem to have even
a passing acquaintance with any public man of
respectable reputation.

In his later works the omissions are more
remarkable still, for by that time his society
was courted by many distinguished by rank, in
letters, or in art. Yet in 'Philip' the publisher
and the authors, if intended to represent a class,
are obvious caricature, and before he wrote
'The Virginians' he must have discovered that
a peer is not of necessity either an idiot or a
sot. But so startling is his attitude towards
some sections of the community, that no ex-
amination of the circumstances of the first
portion of his active life will serve to explain it.
He almost seems to have persisted in certain
views less from habit than perversity. 'Esmond'
could not have been written by any one who in
taste and sympathies was not in himself an
aristocrat, but if one runs over the list of his
noble characters not contained in that volume,
the names that suggest themselves are those of
Lord Bareacres and Lord Crabs, Lord Ringwood, and the Marquises of Steyne and Farintosh. The single exceptions that are not

historical, are Lord Kew in ' The Newcomes,' and
the slightly-drawn characters of Lady Knightsbridge in ' The Kickleburys on the Rhine,' and
Lady Rockminster in ' Pendennis.'

His treatment of the clergy is even more
extraordinary, and the explanation that a man
so reverent would naturally pursue any one
who degraded his sacred office with peculiar
vehemence, would serve better if Thackeray had
been dealing with real and not fictitious personages. After all, it is not so much for the opinions
he holds that an author is responsible, as for
those he actively disseminates, and what an
opinion of the English clergy must the reader,
who is content to take Thackeray at his word,
be compelled to form ! There is a paper on
clerical snobs, and the degrading spectacle of
Mr. Tufton Hunt. There is Bishop Tusher, of
whom it is enough to remark that no worse
punishment could be found for Beatrix than to
marry her to him. Mr. Sampson plays a large
part in ' The Virginians,' and the Rev. C. J.
Honeyman wearies the reader of ' The Newcomes ' with his continual whine. Dr. Portman
in ' Pendennis ' is too slight a sketch to be placed
in opposition to these, and it was not till he

came to write ' Denis Duval ' that Thackeray
did tardy justice to the profession by the creation
of Dr. Barnard.

These are serious faults, and care is needed
lest undue weight should be given them ; but
it must at once be conceded that they afford
some ground for the hasty criticism, that they
are the product of " a club-window view of life."
Catch phrases, however, are apt to mislead ;
they owe their popularity to the attraction
of facile and effective exaggeration, and they
escape criticism the more easily as their meaning is seldom precise. It is not perhaps unfair
that they should be construed with liberality,
and that, where ambiguous, they should be
understood in the most favourable sense ; but
such leniency tends to perpetuate their existence. In the present instance it is so obvious
that Thackeray's view of life was not that of
the ordinary spectator at the window of a club,
that the originator of the phrase must be supposed to have meant something less violent and
false. The ordinary member of a club, passing
from his window his airy judgment on men and
things, is in general a superficial observer, or
at best, but " a surface man of theories, true

to none." If Thackeray had a characteristic
that can be said to be peculiarly his own, it
was his power of seeing into the interior of a
heart, and his habit of analyzing and dissecting
the mechanism of our actions and emotions.
The author of the phrase under discussion
cannot have meant to deny this, and to say
that Thackeray had "a club-window view of
life" must be understood to mean that he saw
life from a club-window, and this, though subject
to deductions, contains a large element of truth.
If we leave 'Esmond' out of account, and put
on one side a variety of characters, of whom
Colonel Newcome, Mrs. Pendennis, Laura, and
Ethel are a few, it will be found to be a sufficiently notable characteristic of his work. He
brought, in short, his great faculties to bear on
an artificially restricted area.

His omissions alone would not justify this
criticism, no author can be expected to deal
with every profession and occupation ; but if
he does deal with many of them, the principle
of selection should not be arbitrary, and those
dealt with should be treated with truth and
care. That the villain of a story should belong
to any particular class may be, and generally

is, an accident, and that Arthur Dimmesdale [1]
should be a clergyman is no libel on the
clergy ; but Thackeray must have known that
his journalists, his aristocrats, and his chaplains
appeal to the public not more as individuals
than as types, not more as men who disgrace
the class to which they belong than as repre-
sentatives of others by supposition similar to
themselves. A novelist, moreover, who ostenta-
tiously offers to conduct us round Vanity Fair,
has no title to miss so many of its important
streets ; and a moralist who expects to convince
should furnish a fair description of a society upon
which he is eager to animadvert ; his auditors
must be assured of the authenticity of the text
before they can become interested in its exposition. That there are wicked people in the world
is unfortunately true,—if it were not so there
would be no need for a moralist,—but the proportion wickedness bears to virtue is exaggerated
in Thackeray's novels quite beyond belief.

But it is not only in dealing with the pre-
valence of vice that his cynicism is apparent ;
an acute critic has pointed out that it is not
quite absent even when he is treating of virtue.

[1] In ' The Scarlet Letter.'

One can imagine what a shout of joy Diogenes
the cynic would have raised if he had satisfied
himself that "he had encountered anywhere an
honest man doing his duty with decent con-
stancy,"[1] and the jubilation in which Thackeray
indulges over the virtues of Colonel Newcome
and Esmond comes dangerously near conveying
a reproach to their species.   It is true that the
turning-point of Esmond's career is occasioned
by an act of self-sacrifice seldom equalled, and
the magnanimity of the Colonel when assailed
by Mrs. Mackenzie is such as almost to be out
of the course of nature ; but there are many of
their ordinary actions which come in for an excessive measure of laudation, and the innuendo
that kindness, simplicity, and affection are no
part of our common lives is not to be overlooked.

These are the limitations which attach to
Thackeray as a novelist and as a moralist, and
the one character suffers from each of them as
much as the other.   The duty of a novelist is
primarily that of an observer, but it is not
possible to observe without forming conclusions
on what has been seen.   The duty of a moralist

---

[1] Carlyle on Savage Landor.   'Conversations with
Carlyle,' Sir Charles Gavan Duffy, K.C.M.G.   1892.

is primarily that of a commentator, but he cannot properly come to a conclusion unless he
has observed. It is necessary to have seen
everything before one can either judge or represent the whole. In so far as one's vision is
restricted one will fall short of excellence in
either capacity. But though this is true, and
the provinces of an artist and a moralist are
identical, they approach the common ground
from different directions. It is the duty of a
moralist to point the moral relations in the
world ; of an artist to show the world in moral
relations. The work of a great artist must be
moral if the world is moral ; his business is to
survey mankind, and to show a small piece of
nature, governed by the same laws which
regulate, and subject to the same conditions
which determine, a whole so vast that, without
his aid, few can understand it. Virtue in his
pages may go unrewarded, vice may flourish in
high places, and he may have to pay no forfeit
to the truth. But if his work is to be artistic, if
his object is not to seize violently, and detach
from its natural setting, any particular portion
of experience ; if his aim, however slight his
sketch, however special his subject, is to repre-

sent a part without prejudice to the whole; virtue and vice, when exhibited, must arouse in the other actors in his tale, in the chorus in his mimic world, the same sentiments which these qualities invariably excite. His characters, unless perfect or diabolical, and such instances in nature are astonishingly few, must possess the vices corresponding to their virtues, and the excellences corresponding to their defects. A warm-hearted man may be represented as a drunkard, but not as both warm-hearted and cruel; a brave soldier as committing murder, but not as the perpetrator of a petty theft. Lastly, Virtue and Vice must appear in their ordinary proportion. The literary artist, in this sense, is the interpreter of Nature, though he is no mere copyist, and his individuality is a factor that properly enters into his criticism of life; but the play of his individuality must not lead him to overstep the limits prescribed for his art. He must neither violate probability, nor misrepresent experience.

Judged by this standard 'Vanity Fair' is immoral just because it is inartistic. The portrayal of the Marquis of Steyne is neither immoral nor inartistic, but the account of his reception by the public of 'Vanity Fair' is both. Mr. Osborne could hardly, at one and the same time, regret his treatment of his son, and carry his resentment towards his son's faithful friend so far beyond the grave. The company brought together in 'Vanity Fair' is an outrage on the constitution of the world. The multitudinous sermons that Thackeray preaches in the novel do not save it from artistic immorality. They prevent its tendency being practically vicious, but by a method foreign to an artist.

This is all the truth to be extracted from the discussion M. Taine has dealt with, at such needless length, and from which he has derived such bewildering conclusions. His famous sentence, "The regular presence of a moral intention spoils the novel," if it means more than what has just been admitted,—and when taken with its context it can hardly be supposed to mean nothing more,—is the exact contrary of the facts. A great artist is a great moralist, whether consciously or not ; and it is impossible to suppose that the moral effect produced by Shakespeare's plays or the novels of Scott is the result of simple accident. The incidents of 'Othello,' of 'Lear,' and of 'Old Mortality,' are so

arranged as to satisfy almost every moral sentiment which we possess. The regular presence
of a moral intention, as a matter of fact, saves
and strengthens the novel. It is only by the
regular presence of a moral intention that any
great work of art is ever produced. It is only
by its regular presence that the public is spared
the infliction of periodical disquisitions upon the
conduct of life. Had 'Vanity Fair' not been,
in this respect, artistically a failure, its readers
might have been left to take care of themselves.
In 'Pendennis,' where the representation of the
world is far more artistic, and consequently far
more true, the constant warnings to avoid the
indolence of Arthur are received with the good-
natured laugh that they provoke. 'The Newcomes' marks a further advance in the proper
function of the moralist in art, and 'Esmond'
is as moral a work as any great artist ever
wrote, but it is precisely because of the moral
idea that pervades it that it is so great an
artistic success. Here the showman no longer
cries his sermon, and we are left at peace to
contemplate, as we turn its pages, the busy
scheme in which, at once as passive and active
forces, our lives are interwoven.

Turning from the discussion as to how far
Thackeray's novels suffer artistically from their
frequent moralizing digressions, and looking at
his morality itself, it is natural to ask :—What
is the value of this message he was so eager
to deliver, these lessons he was so anxious to
inculcate ? The question admits of no very
satisfactory answer. That he was dissatisfied
with the constitution of society is abundantly
evident, and if his contemporaries were as he
has represented them, his counsels would be of
good effect. But he so exaggerates the faults
he reprehends, he so misrepresents the classes
which he professes to reform, that much advice,
admirable in itself, vanishes in the air. No one
who commits the errors he specially detested
is likely to be made better by these sermons
at Cornhill. Such a man, if he happens to
read Thackeray's novels, is more likely to
think that as he is so obviously superior to his
type there represented, he must already be
nearly perfect of his kind. No gambler who
studies the character of Deuceace, no *roué*
who surveys the portrait of Lord Steyne, no
foolish youth who laughs at the foolish talk
of Lord Farintosh, but is able with justice to

repeat, " How much better am I than other men." The result is curious and instructive ; retributive justice has overtaken a great moralist and a great artist who neglected the canons of his art, and it is not in these digressions of which he was fond, and in which the real lover of Thackeray still finds much that is delightful, that the secret of his influence is to be found.

His power consists, as has been said, in his exceptional knowledge of character, in his wonderful mastery over the sources of emotion, and in a view of existence that, with its plaintive note rising from the midst of dignity and self-restraint, has reflected and informed the best thought of our time. Carlyle, the other censor of the age, like Thackeray, was no optimist, but it is curious to mark the difference in their respective positions towards a problem by which more than by any other they were both profoundly stirred—Carlyle alternately storming against the limitations of our mortal condition, and rejecting with a furious contempt the varying solutions of the riddle : Thackeray going over and over again, with an exquisite felicity of phrase, the line of the Roman poet—

" O curas hominum, O quantum est in rebus inane."

yet pointing, with a benign security, to those far-off and "shining table-lands" that rebuke, from their silent distance, the fever of our crowded and important life.

The world will decide which of these attitudes is the more classic—the more loveable.

ADDENDUM

Chronological List of Works mentioned in this Essay.